THE LIVING GARDEN

A PRACTICAL GUIDE TO
GARDENING THE NATURAL WAY

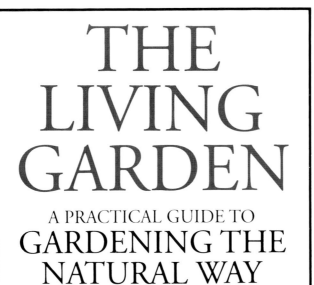

THE LIVING GARDEN

A PRACTICAL GUIDE TO
GARDENING THE
NATURAL WAY

GEOFF HAMILTON
AND JENNIFER OWEN

BBC BOOKS

This book is published to accompany the
television series entitled The Living Garden
which was first broadcast in November 1992

Published by BBC Books,
a division of BBC Enterprises Limited,
Woodlands, 80 Wood Lane,
London W12 0TT

First published 1992

ISBN 0 563 36412 2

Designed by Grahame Dudley Associates
Illustrations by Barbara Hampton

For photograph sources and copyright
information see page 9

Set in Old Style 11/13pt by Selwood Systems,
Midsomer Norton
Printed and bound in Great Britain by
Butler & Tanner Ltd, Frome
Colour separation by Technik Ltd, Berkhamsted
Jacket printed by Lawrence Allen Ltd,
Weston-super-Mare

Contents

CHAPTER FIVE

A HEALTHY PLANT

CHAPTER SIX

POLLINATION – CONTINUING THE LINE

CHAPTER SEVEN

PESTS – THE BANE OF GARDENERS

CHAPTER EIGHT

MANIPULATING NATURE

CHAPTER NINE

PROPAGATION – CAPITALISING ON WHAT YOU'VE GOT

CHAPTER TEN

THE COMPLETE GARDEN

Photo Credits

A–Z Botanical Collection page 110 *top left*; **Pat Brindley** page 173; **Bruce Coleman** pages 20 *top* (Gordon Langsbury), 20 *bottom* (Kim Taylor), 21 (Jane Burton), 28 (Dennis Green), 40 *right* (Jane Burton), 41 *bottom* (Frieder Sauer), 44 *top right* (Jane Burton), 45 (Carmel Galea), 49 *bottom* (Adrian Davies), 60 *top* (Kim Taylor), 72 *top left* (Eric Crichton), 99 *top left* (Hans Reinhard), 107 *bottom right* (Fritz Prenzel), 110 *top right* (John Markham), 115 *bottom left* (Eric Crichton), 115 *bottom right* (Jane Burton), 122 *bottom* (Jane Burton), 133 *bottom* (Kim Taylor), 136 *top right* (John Markham), 141 *top left* (Jane Burton), 141 *bottom left* (J. Brackenbury), 141 *bottom right* (Kim Taylor) & 181 *right* (Jane Burton); **Garden Picture Library** pages 32, 72 *bottom*, 96 *bottom*, 98, 99 *bottom*, 102, 106–7 *left*, 115 *top*, 123, 126, 127, 133 *top*, 137, 145, 152 *top*, 177, 180–1 *left*, 189, 192 & 195 *top left* & *bottom*; **Stephen Hamilton** pages 13, 36, 57 *top*, 60 *bottom*, 64, 68, 85 *top left*, 87, 88, 136 *bottom*, 148, 184–5 & 198–9; **Holt Studios International** page 149 *bottom*; **Horticultural Research International** pages 152 *bottom* & 153; **NHPA** pages 41 *top* (Walter Murray), 57 *bottom* (Stephen Dalton), 65 *bottom* (Ron Fotheringham), 110 *bottom* (Walter Murray), 118 *top* (Stephen Dalton), 122 *top* (M. I. Garwood) & 196 (Stephen Dalton); **OSF** pages 25 (G. A. MacLean), 29 (Colin Milkins), 40 *left* (D. H. Thompson), 44 *top left* (Peter O'Toole), 44 *bottom* (Tim Shepherd), 65 *top* Harold Taylor, 81 *top* (G. I. Barnard), 93 (G. A. MacLean), 97 (Harold Taylor), 118 *bottom* (K. G. Vock), 132 *top right* (John Cooke), 136 *top left* (Ake Lindau) & 144 *top* (J. A. L. Cooke); **Jennifer Owen** pages 72 *top right*, 132 *top left* & 186–7; **Photos Horticultural** pages 16–17, 33, 76, 77, 85 *top right*, 92 *bottom*, 96 *both top*, 99 *top right*, 103, 107 *top right*, 114, 119 *top*, 144 *bottom*, 157 *top*, 165 *both*, 168, 190, 191, 194 & 195 *top right*; **Premaphotos Wildlife** pages 119 *bottom* & 141 *top right*; **Science Photo Library** pages 49 *top* (Dr Jeremy Burgess), 61 (Dr Tony Brain), 81 *bottom* (Dan Guravich), 111 (Dr Jeremy Burgess), 132 *bottom* (David Scharf) & 149 *top* (Martin Dohrn); **Harry Smith Horticultural Photographic Collection** pages 37, 85 *bottom*, 92 *top*, 157 *bottom* & 169.

Introduction

The garden is perhaps the one place left in our modern world where we can get a practical, 'hands-on' experience of nature. As the species which is top of the natural heap, we can use our influence here to affect the millions of other plants and animals which share our space. It's up to us whether we use our powers in a benign or a malign way to benefit or to harass out of existence the living things in the lower orders.

The choice is ours to engage in a war of wills with nature or to play the game by the natural rules. I believe that gardeners would prefer to live in peace and harmony with their fellow creatures and that the very essence of their pastime is to create a kind of natural Arcadia where all is sweetness and light. But, of course, the natural world simply isn't like that.

We all know that the chain of life depends upon one species living off another. When the hawk is hungry its instinct is to kill the mouse and it does so without hesitation and certainly with no pangs of conscience. Likewise, when the mouse needs to eat, it'll devour the complete seed crop of a particular plant with no thought for the survival of that particular species.

Right up at our elevated end of the scale, our farmers will happily drench plants in poisonous sprays to kill every insect in sight in order that our species should survive. We'll kill weeds and wildflowers alike to reduce competition with food plants and, if that destroys the birds that feed on them, well so be it. After all, that's nature; it's a tough world out there and we must be ruthless in order to survive.

The theory has perhaps worked well so far but now we're beginning to see ominous writing on the wall. It's started to dawn on us that we simply can't live in isolation. Just as all levels of the natural order depend on a lower level for their existence, so do we. If we do poison them all out of existence, we simply destroy the very source of our lives.

The one great proviso of our inheritance has always been that with power comes responsibility. Certainly we hold the destiny of every other species in our hands but if we destroy them we destroy ourselves in the process.

Well, there are bright signs on the horizon. With the realisation of our dangerous position, scientific thinking is now seeking other ways of protecting food plants from pests and diseases without actually killing them, and researching alternatives to polluting chemical fertilisers.

It'll be a long and exacting process but we gardeners have no need to wait. With none of the problems of the food producer – monoculture and macro-economics in

particular – we can welcome our natural friends into the garden and observe with delight the perfection of the natural system.

We can live by nature's own rules, interfering only where absolutely necessary – and our prime position entitles us to do that. The result will be a garden of overwhelming natural beauty that buzzes with wildlife and delights, and fascinates us every single day of our lives.

But in order to make it work we need to understand how the system works and what the rules actually are. And that's what this book is all about.

Geoff Hamilton
November 1992

CHAPTER ONE

HOW A GARDEN WORKS

To understand the workings of the natural world, the gardener first has to appreciate that the function of every living thing is to survive to perpetuate its own species. From the humblest form of algae right up the chain to man himself, all living things have evolved and developed often incredibly complex ways to defend themselves and reproduce their own kind. In many cases they do so simply by producing huge numbers of young. But nature is a hard taskmaster.

A small drama that we've all experienced in our gardens is the discovery of the limp, lifeless body of a small, newly-fledged bird. Our immediate reaction is, 'How sad! What a waste! If I'd found it earlier, perhaps I could have saved it.' This feeling arises from the comfortable awareness of how secure and insulated are our lives, with abundant food and continuing medical and social advances in staving off premature death. But our situation is artificial; out there in the 'real' world high birth rates are the norm and high death rates inevitable.

Put in its simplest terms, all animals and plants are selfish. Each individual strives to make the biggest contribution it can to the next generation by producing as many offspring as it can. Animals do this either by producing lots of small eggs which, once they hatch, are 'on their own'; or by producing a few, larger eggs and often then looking after the young. Cabbage moths, whose caterpillars feed on an incredible range of different plants, not just cabbages, are in the first category, blackbirds are in the second.

A female cabbage moth lays about a hundred small eggs, which hatch into tiny caterpillars. That means that a pair of cabbage moths could become 100 in the second year, 5,000 in the third, 250,000 in the fourth, $12\frac{1}{2}$ million in the fifth, and so on.

Less sensational but just as dramatic is the production of blackbirds. Garden blackbirds lay on average three eggs in a clutch, and make at least three nesting attempts in a year. A pair may raise ten or more fledglings a year, with an average of six, so one year's nesting efforts could add at least three pairs of birds to the population. The next generation is potentially nine pairs, then 27, then 81, then 243 pairs, and so on.

To apply the same sort of mathematics to plants is mind-boggling since just one is capable of producing thousands of seeds. And, just in case that's not successful, some have developed other, vegetative, means of reproduction. Any gardener who's battled with the running roots of couch grass or ground elder knows exactly what we mean.

Unless there was some kind of natural control, we'd be overrun by blackbirds, knee-deep in cabbage moths and choking in couch grass in next to no time. This incredible production of new 'bodies' is drastically trimmed down by low survival rates and under normal circumstances animals, and plants too, do no more than replace themselves. The perhaps unwelcome but inescapable truth is that the vast majority of animals and plants that are born, hatch from eggs or are distributed as seed never reach maturity, most of them dying when they're young or, in the case of plants, not germinating at all.

Death is the great regulator that stabilises the numbers of different sorts (or species) of plants and animals, whether they're cabbage moths, blackbirds or couch grass, from one generation to another. This happens because there are too many of them for the environment to support. Perhaps there's insufficient food for all so most starve, or not enough nesting places so few can breed. There may be a shortage of sheltering places so most are killed by bad weather, or few hiding places so the majority are caught and eaten, and so on.

A particular habitat, say a garden, can only support so many of any particular sort of animal or plant. If conditions change, however, so that food, breeding space or something else essential becomes more readily available, there are fewer deaths so numbers rise.

And this is where the gardener can juggle with the conditions to adapt them for his own good. If he wants to grow more or bigger plants in his garden than nature would normally allow he can improve the conditions by adding manure, compost and fertiliser and he can reduce competition by removing those plants he doesn't want. Bear in mind that by pulling out one weed at the right time you prevent the distribution of perhaps a thousand seeds.

Likewise, it's possible to influence the animal life that visits your garden. If nesting sites are limited in the area, you'll increase the number of, say, blue tits by providing them with nesting boxes. But even then there may be disaster, as most of the chicks could die in the nest because there's not enough insect food in the garden. Food has now become what limits the numbers, and death by starvation the regulator, unless the gardener addresses that problem too.

THE LIMITS TO NUMBERS OR TO GROWTH

Whatever essential requirement is in shortest supply is normally the factor which limits the numbers, maybe even the very existence, of an animal or plant. Plants crowded together may not have enough moisture to grow. Irrigate, and most will thrive for a while but many may then die because there's not enough food.

Even the growth of an individual plant is limited by the availability of the essential requirement which is in shortest supply. To make sugars (the chemical process known as photosynthesis) a plant needs water, carbon dioxide, light and a high enough

temperature. Given that a plant has enough water, then increasing the light intensity increases the rate at which it manufactures sugars, but only up to a certain level. However, if you increase the temperature the rate of photosynthesis again increases, but again only up to a certain level. Increase the concentration of carbon dioxide around the plant and again the rate of sugar production goes up. It's a balancing act and the rate of photosynthesis is always limited by whatever is in shortest supply.

Growing plants also need lots of other chemicals such as nitrates, phosphates and potassium salts as food. These three are needed for healthy growth of leaves, roots and flowers but others are also required in minute quantities. Magnesium deficiency, for example, leads to yellowing of leaves, which shows that the plant lacks the green pigment chlorophyll. It's chlorophyll that absorbs light to convert carbon dioxide and water to sugars and without a minute amount of magnesium this won't happen.

Many other chemical elements are required in minute quantities in plants, but are none the less essential. These are the so-called trace elements, such as boron, iron and molybdenum.

COMPETITION – THE STRUGGLE FOR EXISTENCE

Because many more plants and animals are produced than can survive there's a continual struggle for existence which takes the form of competition for whatever is essential to an animal or plant. A blackbird, for instance, competes not only with other blackbirds for food and nesting places but also to some extent with other similar birds.

Colourful gardens such as this one attract many insects to feed.

A rose bush competes both with other roses and also with other sorts of plants for water, space, light and nutrients.

Competition in animals rarely leads to overt aggression and fighting, even between members of the same species. Blackbirds, for example, establish rights to a particular nest site, food source, territory and so on and these are unmistakably advertised by song and attitude. An intruding blackbird visiting a small garden which another pair regard as their territory, and which probably could support only one pair, is soon seen off.

Blackbirds are unlikely to compete with totally different birds such as blue tits because they eat different food, nest in different places, and generally use the environment in different ways. But what happens when several closely related and hence similar species are using the same habitat? After all, their demands on the environment are bound to be more or less the same.

Blackbirds have one close relative, the song thrush, usually present in gardens; another, the mistle thrush, that is often present; and two further close relatives, redwings and fieldfares, that visit in winter. All five are similar in size and structure, and all eat berries and other fruit, worms, snails, insects and spiders. But it's as though they have partitioned the environment, the space and the food it contains between them so that no two species ultimately depend on the same essential resource.

Fieldfares and redwings are winter visitors to Britain, breeding in northern continental Europe, and mistle thrushes require large trees in well-wooded areas for breeding.

In winter, these three visit gardens to feed on fallen apples, on holly and other berries, and in hard winters when food is scarce they will rootle through leaf litter for insects and other small animals. But they rarely compete with the predominantly animal-eating resident song thrushes and blackbirds.

Slight-size differences, particularly in the gape of the beak lead to differences in the size of berries they can best cope with. Song thrushes eat snails whenever they are available, breaking the shells on 'anvil' stones, and are adept at locating and extracting earthworms from lawns. Blackbirds, however, are opportunists, eating whatever they can get hold of, whether it be caterpillars, worms turned up by the gardener's spade, ant grubs and pupae tipped out of unused seed trays in the greenhouse, or food scraps washed down into the kitchen drain.

Similar though the five species are, competition seems to be averted by the way they have specialised in slightly different ways.

THE WEB OF LIFE

For most animals, of course, life is made up not only of finding food but also of avoiding being eaten. All animals and plants slot into food-chains.

Cabbages, for example, are eaten by mealy-looking cabbage aphids, which are in turn eaten by the legless, flattened larvae of several sorts of yellow-and-black-banded hoverflies. The adult hoverflies may then be ensnared right on the cabbage leaves by a small, pale, long-legged spider and the spider itself pecked up by a robin.

Perhaps the robin may then fall prey to a cat but even without this event we have a food-chain (cabbage – aphid – hoverfly – spider – bird) along which nutrients and energy pass.

When you harvest the cabbage, trim away

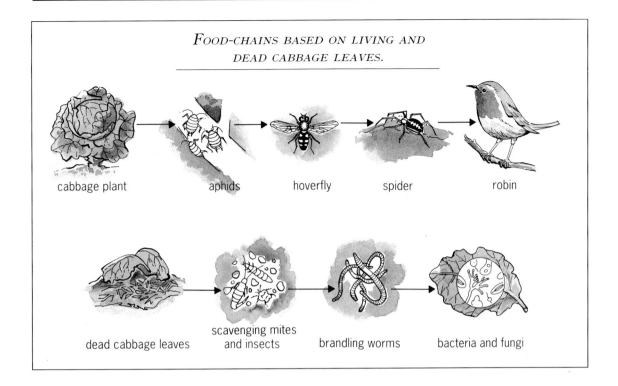

FOOD-CHAINS BASED ON LIVING AND DEAD CABBAGE LEAVES.

cabbage plant   aphids   hoverfly   spider   robin

dead cabbage leaves   scavenging mites and insects   brandling worms   bacteria and fungi

the outer leaves and discard them on the compost heap, another food-chain comes into effect, this time of decomposers, which feed on plants and animals after they're dead.

As rain softens the cabbage leaves and they sink into the refuse of the compost heap, mites and tiny insects nibble at them. Their corpses contribute to the organic melting-pot of the compost heap on which brandlings and other earthworms feed. When they die, bacteria and fungi, which invade all the dead organic material in the compost heap, decompose their remains.

Thus, once the cabbage is dead, its nutrients and energy pass along another food-chain (cabbage – scavenging mites and insects – brandlings – bacteria and fungi).

But it's not quite as straightforward as that. Although you can recognise food-chains in your garden, they're usually complicated by the fact that any particular animal or plant is eaten by a variety of different sorts of animals, and most animals eat a range of different foods.

Cabbages are chewed by the caterpillars of moths and cabbage white butterflies, nibbled at by flea beetles, and sucked by whitefly and spittlebugs as well as by aphids. Aphids are parasitised by tiny wasps, and eaten by a whole range of birds and wasps, by ladybirds and lacewing larvae, as well as by hoverfly larvae.

Hoverflies are eaten by many different sorts of birds, even by swifts circling high in the air above the garden. They're also captured by wasps as food for their young, and they're parasitised and consumed by other smaller wasps, as well as being caught by spiders.

Spiders are eaten by many different sorts of birds, are caught by wasps to feed their young, and they and their eggs are parasitised by tiny wasps. Evidently, the

Above left, *redwings visit in winter to feed on berries;* **left**, *song thrushes crack snail shells on favourite 'anvil-stones';* **above**, *a garden spider hangs in the middle of her web.*

plant and animals in our food-chain may be eaten by lots of different animals.

Looking at it from the opposite perspective, most animals also have a varied diet. Hoverfly larvae eat many different sorts of aphids on different plants, as well as other small, plant-sucking bugs. And when they grow up to be adult hoverflies their diet will be a vegetarian one of nectar and pollen from flowers.

Spiders suck juices from any small animal they can capture, including other spiders, and robins eat all sorts of insects from beetles to moths, centipedes and earthworms, as well as spiders. But, though predominantly animal-feeders, robins also take weed seeds, berries and soft fruit. We have in our gardens, or anywhere else, not so much a series of food-chains, as a vast interlocking food-web, a great mesh of feeding activities.

We can't even keep the animals that eat living things separate from those that eat them after they're dead. Earthworms are decomposers, consuming dead organic matter in the soil, but blackbirds will eat them as readily as they'll eat caterpillars feeding on living green plants. Bacteria and fungi in the soil break down all dead tissue, whether it comes from earthworms, hoverflies, spiders, birds or the leaves of cabbages. Eating and being eaten connects in one way or another all the plants and animals in a garden into a giant network.

Other cross-connections in the food web arise from the way many animals eat different things when they're developing and when they're adult. We've already mentioned hoverflies and wasps. Most of the common hoverflies in gardens eat aphids as larvae. As adults, however, they feed at flowers, taking both pollen and nectar. Even this is not straightforward, because they tend to feed on any sweet fluids that they find, and lap up honeydew excreted by aphids, juices from fermenting fruits, and even liquids oozing from rotting carcasses.

Not all hoverflies prey on aphids as larvae. Different species feed on plants, on tree sap, on decaying and semi-liquid organic material, whether it be of plant or animal origin, and scavenge in bee and wasp nests, eating corpses, excrement, litter and sometimes the live grubs. All, however, when they become adult, feed on pollen, nectar and other sweet fluids.

Wasps, similarly, eat very differently as young and as adults. As adults both the common yellow and black social wasps and the many different sorts of solitary wasps lap up nectar, fruit juices and other sweet fluids. But their larvae need an animal diet, and the adults hunt for this to provide for their young.

Social wasps chew the caterpillars, spiders and other animals they catch into sort of hamburger pellets, which they take back to their large, round nests and feed to their grubs. Solitary wasps stock their holes with prey – aphids, flies, caterpillars, or spiders (depending on the species of wasp) – and deposit on it an egg which, when it hatches into a grub, consumes the conveniently situated food. So, though we gardeners may complain that wasps damage our ripe fruit we should perhaps console ourselves with the knowledge that they control pests too.

One-way energy transfer

Another way of looking at this feeding network is as a complex of inter-connecting pathways along which energy flows. The cabbage plant, for example, manufactures sugars during photosynthesis using carbon dioxide and water, and taking energy from the sun. The energy used is effectively stored in the sugars, some being used in the plant's

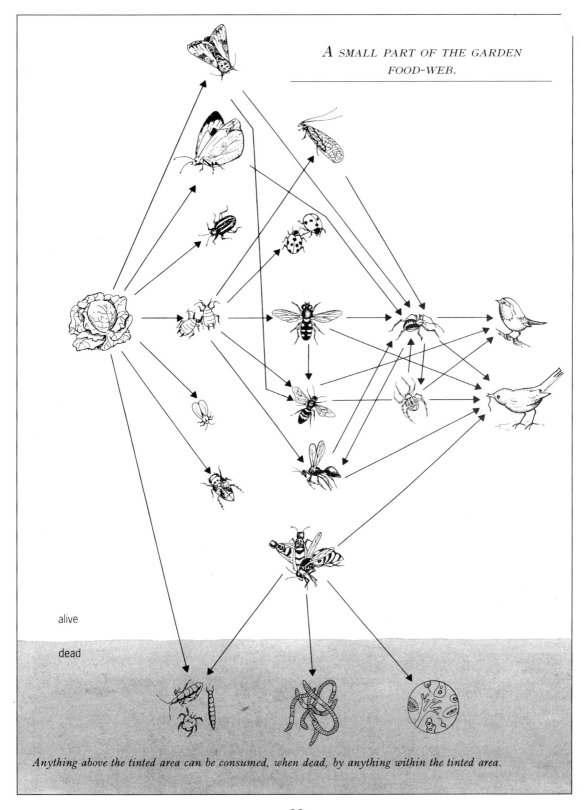

A SMALL PART OF THE GARDEN
FOOD-WEB.

alive

dead

Anything above the tinted area can be consumed, when dead, by anything within the tinted area.

life processes, but about 80 per cent being stored as chemical energy in the plant.

When aphids feed on the cabbage leaves they take on this stored chemical energy. They use much of it in their own bodily activities, and this is eventually lost as heat, but some is stored in their tissues. This stored energy goes to the hoverfly larvae that eat the aphids; again much is used and lost as heat and the rest stored. So on, through spider and bird, some of the chemical energy in the food is used and a small proportion is stored in the tissues. Plant-eaters (herbivores) and animal-eaters (carnivores) store only between 5 and 20 per cent of the energy content of their food, the rest is used in living and eventually lost as heat.

This means that in our example of a food-chain (cabbage – aphid – hoverfly – spider – bird) the amount of stored energy available to the bird, and particularly to the cat that may eat the bird, is very small. That's why so-called top predators – the last link in the food-chains – are always rare compared with aphids and other herbivores that feed directly on plants.

The inefficiency of this one-way energy transfer between different links in food-chains sets an upper limit to the length of

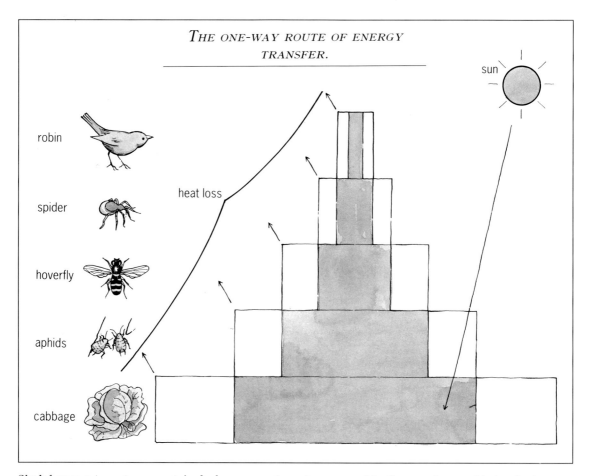

THE ONE-WAY ROUTE OF ENERGY TRANSFER.

sun

robin

heat loss

spider

hoverfly

aphids

cabbage

Shaded areas represent energy retained; clear areas represent energy used by the organisms and lost as heat.

Wasps drink sweet fluids but catch caterpillars and other soft-bodied animals to feed their young.

food-chains. The majority have just three links.

RECYCLING: THE NUTRIENTS CYCLE

The pathway of nutrients is very different from the one-way energy pathway because they're not used up or lost. Instead they're recycled and used again and again.

The nitrogen, phosphorus, potassium, calcium, sulphur or any other element taken up in the form of mineral salts from the soil by plant roots is built up into the material of the plant. When the plant is eaten by an animal these substances are reassembled as animal tissue. When one animal eats another, the same reassembling takes place; nothing is lost.

When an animal or plant dies or produces waste, all eventually decomposes and the constituent elements are released in the soil as nitrates, phosphates, sulphates and so on. Then they are once again available to plants and can again pass through the food-chain.

It's recycling *par excellence* with no waste. Everything is used again and again – a valuable lesson for the gardener. Just think, your cabbages, and even you yourself, may contain atoms of nitrogen or calcium that were once part of a mammoth that roamed Britain thousands of years ago or, going even further back, a dinosaur.

COMMUNITY MATTERS

The worms that work your soil, the trees that shade the patio, the bees that pollinate your gooseberries, the hedgehog that rootles for insects in the hedge bottom, the ladybirds eating aphids on the runner beans, the swifts wheeling in the air above, are all parts of the inter-relating and interlocking community of animals and plants that live in your garden habitat. Interfere with one

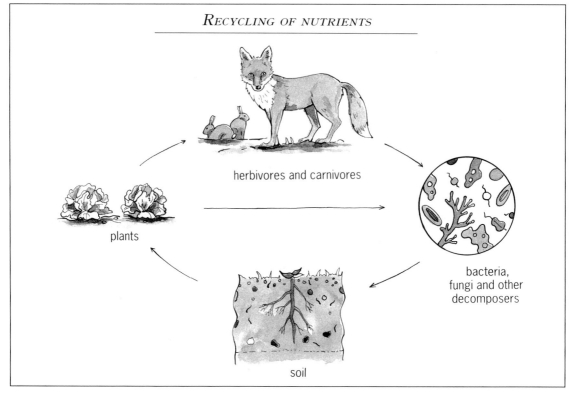

RECYCLING OF NUTRIENTS

herbivores and carnivores

plants

bacteria, fungi and other decomposers

soil

Recycling of nutrients which go round and round from plants through animals and decomposers to the soil, and so back to plants.

element in this mosaic and there will be repercussions throughout.

Most inter-relationships in a community are food-based, though not all. Nesting great tits and blue tits use holes in trees; blackbirds, linnets and many others lodge their nests on tree branches or in the woody tangle of a shrub; and birds of many sorts collect twigs, dry grass or other plant material for their nests.

A wren, for example, builds several relatively enormous, domed, enclosed nests as part of its courtship ritual, only one of which is actually used for eggs. The nests are woven from dead grass, such leaves as montbretia, and clumps of saxifrage and other matted plant material. The whole structure is wedged into hedges or worked into the twining stems of climbers like

honeysuckle against a fence, and the outside is covered with moss and decorated with flowers. Such a bird is inter-relating with many different plants in the community. Have a 'tidy-up' and you could be depriving it of vital building materials, or even destroying its building plot.

Many solitary wasps nest in holes in plant stems or tree-trunks but none bores its own holes. Some use hollow stems but others use holes and tunnels bored by beetles so their presence and breeding success is dependent upon the beetles.

Bumble-bees often establish colonies in the abandoned nests of field mice, voles and shrews, using the hollowed-out ball of dried grass and leaves that the small mammal accumulated as nesting material. The buff-tailed bumble-bee and one of the red-tailed black bumble-bees use abandoned mouse nests approached by an underground tunnel several feet long. Interdependence of bumble-bees and small mammals is close. The garden is a network not only of feeding activities but also of lodgers, for many small animals live in the nests of other creatures.

CLOSING THE CIRCLE

As gardeners we can improve our efficiency and success if we appreciate the way the garden works. In the ecosystem we're interested in – the garden – an enormous subsidy in the form of energy is contributed by the gardener. Without our constant effort our plots of land would soon revert to natural vegetation and lose their order and pattern.

Everything you put into your garden can be 'costed' in terms of energy and expressed in Calories, familiar to slimmers as units of energy content. (One Calorie is the heat needed to raise the temperature of a kilogram of water by one degree Celsius.)

Whenever you apply chemical fertiliser to your vegetable patch or use an insecticidal spray against aphids, the garden receives an energy subsidy equivalent to the energy used to manufacture, transport and apply the chemicals. Similarly, watering the vegetable patch, making and spreading compost, weeding to reduce competition, felling a tree to increase the availability of light, and all the hundred and one tasks that occupy a gardener, add up to a massive energy subsidy.

The good news about this energy balance sheet is that this massive input allows a massive output, and that is exactly what we gardeners expect in return for our efforts. Every flower we cut for the living room, every vegetable harvested for the kitchen, every log burnt on the hearth, is a justified dividend, representing nutrients and chemical energy exported from the system. But there is no reason why the subsidy should exceed the dividends, so it makes sense to keep the subsidy as small as possible.

That's why it's logical to compost as much garden 'rubbish' as possible rather than burning it or carting it off to the tip. That would just be squandering the profits of the garden system rather than making it work for you, and the losses would have to be made good by a massive injection of nutrients and the energy needed to recycle them. Let the garden work for you and you can manage with a less costly subsidy.

We can't increase the input of light energy to our gardens but, by feeding the soil and using plenty of compost, we can ensure that plant growth is limited only by the availability of light rather than of nitrogen or some other nutrient.

The more chemical energy is stored in plants the better chance there is of plant-eaters and animal-eaters being well-represented in a garden. The more nutrients and energy move through the system, the richer the garden fauna is likely to be. Because many plant-eaters are finicky about just what they eat, growing a diverse collection of garden plants results in a more diverse array of animals.

But you might think that encouraging lots of animals in the garden including the plant-feeders, leads to chewing and defoliation of garden plants. It doesn't, mainly because most herbivores are so choosy. Newly-hatched caterpillars, for example, can cope with only the freshest, softest and most tender green leaves. So, caterpillars that feed on one or just a few plant species find that food is in very short supply.

If a plant species 'allowed' itself to be

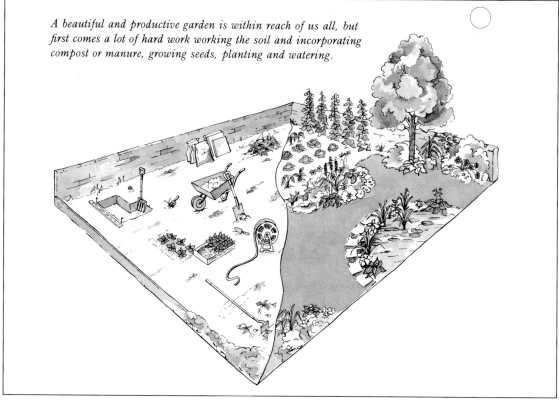

A beautiful and productive garden is within reach of us all, but first comes a lot of hard work working the soil and incorporating compost or manure, growing seeds, planting and watering.

Above left, *the nesting success of blackbirds is high in gardens;* **left**, *creating a beautiful and productive garden means a lot of hard work but the rewards are great;* **above**, *a wood mouse eating a crocus benefits from vitamin A in the saffron of the stigma.*

eaten entirely by animals it could not flower, seed and reproduce itself. The plant species would die out and so would any animal that depended on it. It would be disastrous for caterpillars or aphids to devour or drain a tree because in the long term they and their progeny need the whole tree. So, despite the apparent superabundance of plant food, plant-eaters are limited in numbers by the availability of the right sort of food. There may be many different sorts of herbivore in a garden, but as long as there is great plant diversity and a balance of life that includes predators as well as pests, none is likely to get out of hand.

But, as the 'top' species, why should we not use our technology to control, at least partially, plant-eaters we don't want in the garden? Well, the fact is that the food and energy chains are so complex that the whole ecosystem of the garden is very sensitive to pollution. Persistent poisons in the form of herbicides or insecticides often move unaltered through the food- and energy-chains, accumulating to lethal levels in predators and contaminating the soil.

An insecticidal spray used against aphids is concentrated many times in each of the hoverflies that eat them. It's concentrated further in the swifts soaring above the garden and eating the hoverflies. And when aphids, hoverflies or swifts die, the chemicals may be released into the soil, interfering with the efficiency of bacteria essential for recycling.

The garden operates as a complicated, dynamic network and the functioning of every part of it is influenced in some way, however small, by the presence and activities of the rest. Any interference with its operation is fraught with danger and will almost certainly create more problems than it was intended to solve.

CHAPTER TWO

THE SOIL AND HOW TO IMPROVE IT

Soil is the very basis of human life. What some unenlightened folk call 'dirt' is essential to our very existence since all of our food comes ultimately from the soil. So it's deserving of our utmost respect. Many peoples considered more 'primitive' than us hold the earth in such awe that they treat it as a deity because, unlike us, they have not forgotten that from it springs all of life.

Soil is the gardener's raw material and its fertility will affect the health and productivity of everything you grow. But just what is this thing we call 'fertility'? Why is it that some soils will produce bumper crops of flowers, fruit and vegetables while others are hard and unyielding?

Well, of course, man has been trying to discover the secrets of fertility since we stopped hunting and gathering our food and began to cultivate it. Nature has all the answers and if you just follow the natural rules fertility will follow, and healthy, heavy-yielding plants with it. But we

gardeners have to remember that we expect to take out much, much more than nature ever intended. So, though we would be wise to do things nature's way, we have to increase our input to the soil many times.

THE FORMATION OF SOIL

The mineral particles that form the inorganic bulk of soil have been produced from rocks over millions of years by physical and chemical weathering. Rocks have been split and broken by such events as the freezing and thawing of water percolating into cracks. Wind, sea and rivers have ground them down and as their fragments have been swirled together by water or moved around by wind they've been broken and ground into smaller and smaller particles. Glaciers may have had an effect, grinding rock over rock as they move along, rivers have scoured their beds, and the sea has gnawed at the coast.

Coupled with this physical weathering has been the chemical effect of rainwater and groundwater. These are often weakly acidic solutions of atmospheric carbon dioxide which dissolve out minerals. Clay soils, in particular, are formed by the action of weak acids which change the mineral composition of rock.

Soils, once formed, have often been moved around by the action of glaciers and rivers so that they come to lie over rock different from that which formed them.

For instance, large areas of the Midlands in England are overlain by a thick layer of boulder clay carried there from further north in the last glaciations. River valleys contain alluvial soils washed from upriver to spill out at the river's mouth to form a fertile delta.

Such moving around of soils sifts and sorts the mineral particles on the basis of their size, producing soils with different textures according to the proportions of differently-sized particles they contain.

Sand particles are the largest, 0.02 to 2.0 millimetres in diameter; silt particles are 0.002 to 0.02 millimetres in diameter; clay particles are the smallest at less than 0.002 millimetres in diameter.

SAND, CLAY, SILT AND LOAM

What we call sandy soil contains a high proportion of sand particles and is dry and light and feels gritty when rubbed between the fingers. It's easy to work and warms up quickly in spring but, as it's free-draining, nutrients tend to get washed out.

At the other extreme, clay, with many very small particles, forms a heavy, cold soil which feels sticky when moist and hard and compacted when dry. It doesn't drain easily and is difficult to work when wet but

Most soils are alkaline and many plants, such as Alstroemeria, *prefer a chalky or alkaline soil.*

Rhododendrons and azaleas will not tolerate anything other than an acid soil. It is not easy to increase the acidity of an alkaline soil but incorporating organic matter like cocoashell helps as does sulphur.

is often well supplied with nutrients. It can be turned into a very workable soil by digging, liming and incorporating organic matter.

Silt is intermediate, smooth and silky to the touch, although it has a tendency to pack down when wet, becoming as cold, heavy and badly drained as clay. Its texture can be improved by applying liberal quantities of well-rotted compost or manure.

Loam is the stuff that gardeners' dreams are made of and it's what you'll find in most gardens. It consists of a mixture of particles of different sizes and varies from a light, sandy loam to a heavy clay loam.

You can get some idea of the changes involved in soil formation by digging a flat-sided hole in a relatively undisturbed area such as grassland, going as deep as you can. The vertical sides of the hole will be a soil profile, with unchanged 'parent rock' at the bottom, overlain by slightly changed and eroded mineral matter, known as 'sub-soil', lacking any organic material. On top will be a darker brown layer of 'top-soil' which incorporates a lot of organic matter in the form of decomposing remains of dead plants and animals.

Only the top-soil is of use to the gardener. If you have a garden around a newly-built house you need to make sure that the builder hasn't removed it all, leaving you with infertile sub-soil.

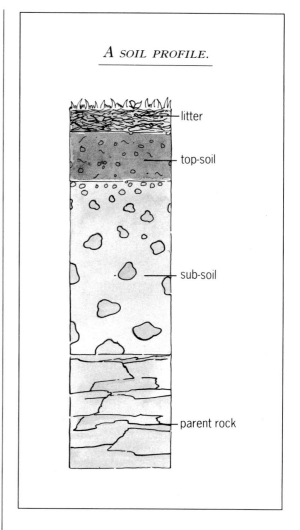

A SOIL PROFILE.

— litter

— top-soil

— sub-soil

— parent rock

IMPROVING THE SOIL

Top-soil, the stuff that the gardener thinks of as his growing medium, contains that necessary ingredient for plant growth – organic matter. Under natural conditions, say in a forest, it comes from dead leaves and ground vegetation, fallen branches, and the corpses of the many animals, large and small, that fed on the vegetation or on each other.

The surface layer of litter continues to provide food for small insects and mites, worms, bacteria and fungi and gradually gets incorporated into the soil, where micro-organisms such as bacteria and soil fungi continue to work on it.

Sugars, starch, cellulose and other substances in dead plant material are broken down fairly quickly by bacteria and fungi. Finally only lignin, the compound that gives wood its tough, fibrous composition, remains.

About 10 per cent of the surface litter in a forest is incorporated into the soil as that magic and important substance humus, which is a complex, organic material composed of lignin plus nitrogen compounds.

Humus is slowly decomposed by micro-organisms but, as it's constantly replaced from litter, the proportion of humus in the soil remains unchanged from year to year. It's a vital constituent of fertile soil, not only as a source of nutrients, but also because it binds mineral particles together, giving that crumbly texture we gardeners all strive for.

Our aim of a fertile soil can only be achieved by maintaining the humus content. It's vital both for feeding plants and also for giving good structure so that there is aeration and drainage, and plant roots grow easily and healthily. In a garden where all dead plant material is cleared away and destroyed, the soil quality eventually deteriorates as its humus content is depleted.

Extra nutrients can be added in the form of chemical fertilisers but this will do nothing for the soil structure. Much can be achieved by allowing dead plant material to accumulate on the soil surface but the best course is to dig quantities of compost into the soil to replenish its humus content. This allows natural decomposition to take place in the soil and is the way things work in nature.

SOIL, WATER AND DRAINAGE

Humus helps to give soil a structure by binding together mineral particles into small lumps or 'crumbs'. Within the crumbs are minute spaces between the mineral particles, often called 'pores', which contain air and water. The pores are much smaller in clay than in sandy soil. There are also spaces between the crumbs and complex of pores within and bet crumbs that makes a well-structur

The spaces, whether filled by air are also home to the millions of tiny organisms on which fertility depends. better the structure of soil, the more humus it will contain, so the less likely it is to drain too rapidly, like sand, or become boggy, like clay. If it has lots of humus, it'll soak up and hold water without becoming waterlogged.

There are various ways you can improve the drainage of your soil, whether the drainage is poor, as with clay, peat and sometimes silt, or too good, as with sandy or chalky soil.

Improving drainage

Because the tiny clay particles were in part formed chemically, it's possible to bind them together chemically in a process known as 'flocculation'. Adding lime binds the particles together to form much larger crumbs but, of course, you have to bear in mind that this will make for a more limey soil and so influence what plants you can grow.

Incorporation of coarse grit at one to two bucketfuls per square metre also helps on clay and silt soils.

Raising the level of the beds, whether on clay or silt, by the deep-bed method (see pages 66–7) also helps. It's more often used when you are growing vegetables but there's no reason not to use it for growing ornamentals.

If you have an intractable problem with bad drainage, as sometimes happens on peaty soil, you may have to use more drastic methods. The main problem with a waterlogged soil is that water fills all the soil pores and spaces, excluding air. The

Digging in compost is the best way of improving the soil and maintaining its humus content.

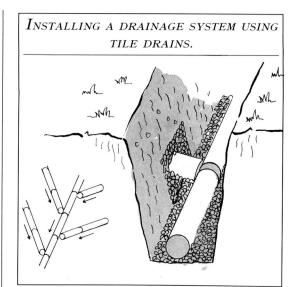

INSTALLING A DRAINAGE SYSTEM USING TILE DRAINS.

Lay the tile drains on a bed of gravel to form a continuous run. Cover the pipes with about 10 cm (4 in) of gravel and then refill the trench with soil. The water seeps in through the spaces left between the pipes.

bacteria responsible for making nitrogen available to plants as nitrates require oxygen and so don't operate in waterlogged soil. Worse than that, another group of bacteria which uses nitrates as a source of energy, breaking them down to nitrogen gas in the process, doesn't require oxygen and thrives in waterlogged soil, which consequently quickly loses its fertility.

So in the worst cases, when incorporation of grit or raising beds is not enough, you may have to build a drainage system. This means digging a herring-bone system of trenches about 45 cm (18 in) deep, sloping gently towards an outlet. In the trenches pack a 15 cm (6 in) layer of stones or twiggy material and cover with soil or, better still, bury tile drains on a bed of gravel to form a continuous run. But the perennial problem is where do you drain the water to? If you have no ditch at the bottom of your garden you could ask your local council if you can run it into their storm drains. But, be warned, it could cost quite a bit.

Reducing drainage

If your soil is sandy or chalky, and drainage is too good, you run the risks not only that plants will be deprived of water but also that essential nutrients will be washed out. This is called leaching. Nutrients are only available to plants in solution and this, of course, is just the form in which they can be washed out of the soil. Too-rapid drainage can be slowed down by digging in bulky organic matter and/or spreading it on the surface. There won't be an overnight improvement but over the years the soil structure will improve and drainage slow down. Organic matter will also help to raise the acidity of the soil so it's doubly valuable on chalky soil.

LIFE IN THE SOIL

Well structured, adequately drained, well aerated, fertile soil will always abound with animals and other organisms. Some will be

Roses do well on clay and silt soils but do not attract many insect visitors.

so large you can't miss them, others are microscopic, but they all play their part in creating and maintaining the fertility of the soil.

Earthworms

Of prime importance for decomposition of dead material and for the maintenance of soil structure (and of inestimable value to the gardener) are earthworms. Not only do they chew up, distribute, bury and eat dead leaves but they plough and work the soil too.

There are several common garden species, one of the most familiar being the large, fat *Lumbricus terrestris*. This makes permanent burrows into which it drags dead leaves and twigs, often leaving some protruding from the burrow entrance. This species has been shown to remove more than 90 per cent of annual leaf fall in an apple orchard during the following winter, amounting to more than a ton of dry leaf weight per hectare (2.47 acres).

Unlike most other animals, earthworms digest cellulose, the stuff of plant cell walls, and consequently make the most of dead plant material as food, but they bury more than they eat, which leads to improved soil fertility. The burrowing of earthworms aerates soil and enhances drainage and so improves conditions for plants and for the all-important bacteria, fungi and other micro-organisms.

Earthworms probably have the greatest effect on the structure of soil by eating it. They're eating excavators, burrowing by sucking soil in through their mouths, digesting much of its organic component, and excreting a mixture of finely-divided soil, leaf fragments and mucus, familiar to us as worm casts. Many sorts of earthworms make worm casts within their burrows,

where they help to establish the crumb structure of soil.

Some species abundant in gardens back up their burrows to make castings on the soil surface, those of the species called *Allolobophora longa* often being conspicuous on lawns. Gardeners and groundsmen all too often regard the castings as a nuisance and the earthworms that produce them as pests but it's evidence of valuable underground activity. Moreover, by eating soil and making surface casts worms bring fine soil particles and nutrients to the surface. If you take particular pride in your lawn, don't try to eradicate the worms, whatever you do; just take a walk around the grass before mowing and disperse any worm casts with a broom, so that the fine soil and nutrients benefit the turf. It's pretty silly to get rid of the worms and then spend hours spiking with a fork to improve aeration.

The nineteenth-century naturalist Charles Darwin was fascinated by earthworms and studied them in his Kent garden and nearby. He worked out that earthworms living in old pasture deposit a soil layer 5 millimetres ($\frac{1}{5}$ inch) thick on the surface every year. He realised that by burrowing and casting, they have a long-term effect in burying stones. His own words on the value of earthworms to the gardener are worth quoting:

Worms prepare the ground in an excellent manner for the growth of fibrous-rooted plants and for seedlings of all kinds. They periodically expose the mould to the air, and sift it so that no stones larger than the particles which they can swallow are left in it. They mingle the whole intimately together, like a gardener who prepares fine soil for his choicest plants. In this state it is well fitted to retain moisture and to absorb all soluble substances, as well as for the process of nitrification.

Moles

There are many other different sorts of animals large enough to be visible and obvious in the soil. One of the largest is the mole, a warm-blooded mammal like ourselves. Moles dig extensive branching systems of burrows with the aid of their large paddle-shaped front feet, an activity that helps to aerate and work the soil.

However, gardeners, groundsmen and farmers regard moles as pests, not least because of the molehills they throw up. They're made from soil excavated from hunting burrows which are usually dug out at a depth of about 10–20 centimetres (4–8 inches). Moles catch and eat many of the animals they encounter while digging these burrows, mainly earthworms but also beetle and fly larvae, snails and millipedes – and they're not above taking small frogs and young mice.

Moles are fascinating and attractive little creatures with dense, silky-soft fur that stands out at right angles to the body so that they can easily move forwards and backwards in their burrows. They certainly work and aerate the soil but, as they are hunters and therefore carnivores, they contribute nothing directly to decomposition of dead plants and recycling of nutrients.

Beetles, centipedes and other animals

Other smaller but still visible animals are also burrowers, moving through the soil

MOLE BURROWS AND A NEST PACKED WITH HAY AND LEAVES.

Molehills consist of the soil excavated from hunting burrows, where moles catch earthworms, beetle larvae and other soil animals. Usually only one mole lives in an extensive burrow system. They store earthworms immobilised by biting to eat during the winter when they are less active.

The big earthworm Lumbricus terrestris *comes to the surface at night and in wet weather. After feeding, they excrete large wormcasts.*

Left, L. terrestris *burrow deep into the soil, particularly in dry weather. They burrow by eating soil.*

creating their own space. Several sorts of beetles and their larvae live in the soil, particularly in the upper layers, eating a range of food. Some are predators of other soil animals while others, like the notorious chafer grubs, are plant-eaters. Some bury and eat dung and others feed on dead plant or animal matter and so contribute directly to decomposition.

A few species of centipede can burrow, although most live in cracks and crevices in the soil. Most are carnivorous although a few eat decaying plant material. Millipedes, in contrast (distinguishable from centipedes because they're round rather than flattened and have many more pairs of legs), are mainly feeders on decaying plant material. They seem to contribute little to its chemical

Above, *moles are rapid and expert burrowers using their powerful front legs for digging.*

Below, *ground beetles are useful predators. This species digests prey externally then sucks up the fluids.*

breakdown but are important in physically breaking it down.

Damper soils may contain many different kinds of fly maggots, most of them eating dead animal matter, although there are some that eat dead plant material, dung, living roots, fungi or other soil animals. Few fly larvae can burrow, being dependent on existing cracks and crevices in the soil.

Ants are much more important as workers of soil. Many species, including the garden black ant, make extensive underground excavations and so bring soil to the surface. Some species, such as wood ants which make large surface mounds, bring considerable quantities of mineral matter from below ground to the surface and this is believed to contribute to the development of crumb structure in the soil.

Most common ants in gardens in Britain eat other animals, either alive or dead, and they may be responsible for concentrating organic matter in the form of faeces and detritus in the soil in their underground nests. Garden black ants may chew through or damage plant roots in the course of their burrowing activities. This is not because they're eating them but rather treating them as obstructions to be removed. Most gardens have black ants in their millions, and you may also find in your garden little yellow ants and bigger red ants, which have a painful bite.

Perhaps the gardeners' greatest enemy is the slug and there are several sorts of slugs, together with small snails, which live in the soil. There are also species that feed on the surface and move down into the soil at other times. Many feed on live plants, rasping away at them with their unique toothed tongue (called a radula); others prefer dead and decaying vegetation. Some eat fungi, others lichens, and a few are carnivorous, eating earthworms or other slugs and snails.

They all play a part in moving organic matter down into the soil and, as they digest cellulose, contribute considerably to the chemical breakdown of plant material. Everyone is familiar with the way slugs and snails produce slime or mucus, left as slime trails on paths, and this material contributes to the crumb structure of soils, by binding particles together.

Soil also contains vast numbers of tiny nematode worms and potworms (enchytraeids). Many nematodes feed on living material such as plant roots, tiny animals, bacteria or fungi, and some are decomposers, feeding on decaying animal or plant matter.

Potworms eat plant fragments as well as bacteria and fungi. They're related to earthworms and, like earthworms, their feeding and excreting contributes to the crumb structure of soil. The fine material excreted by potworms, like the casts of earthworms, stimulates the growth and feeding activities of soil bacteria and fungi.

Woodlice are often present in large numbers and live on the soil surface. Many gardeners believe they damage plants but in fact they mostly feed on dead and decomposing material, usually of plant origin, and they play an important role in breaking up dead material.

Fertile soils teem with a wide range of tiny to microscopic insects, such as springtails, and mites. Springtails eat substantial quantities of dead plant and animal material and their main role is physically breaking up litter.

Mites are the most numerous of all soil animals, present in many hundreds of different species. Many prey on other tiny soil animals, some eat dung, some eat fungi or other plants, and others feed on dead and decaying plant or animal material. Again, their main role seems to be in the physical breakdown of dead matter in the soil.

The breaking down of dead material into smaller fragments is a most important role of soil organisms because it's the tiniest fragments that microscopic bacteria and fungi use as food, breaking them down chemically.

There are also microscopic single-celled animals (Protozoa) and microscopic, often single-celled, plants (algae) in the soil, but it's the bacteria and fungi that are most involved in decomposing dead material.

Bacteria and fungi

These are the real powerhouse of decomposition and recycling and they're incredibly abundant. Bacteria exist as separate cells of various shapes whereas fungi form a mesh, called a mycelium, composed of thread-like structures known as hyphae which spread out between soil particles. The growing tips of the hyphae penetrate dead organic matter liberating digestive enzymes, and sugars and other nutrients are absorbed over the whole mycelium.

It's virtually impossible to recognise a fungus individual because the threads become intertwined, forming a living network in the soil. The only time you'll guess they're there is when the fruiting part of the fungus pushes above the ground as a toadstool.

The soil immediately round plant roots, forming a layer a few millimetres thick, is often bound in a sticky substance which comes from the roots. This layer is a particularly favourable habitat for bacteria, and it's here that they set to work releasing nutrients for the plant.

The importance of the larger animals, from earthworms to springtails, in breaking down dead material so that it's accessible to bacteria and fungi can be demonstrated by burying leaf litter in bags made of different-sized mesh. Leaves in bags of mesh so fine as to admit only micro-organisms show no sign of breakdown even after nine months, whereas decomposition is well advanced in coarse mesh bags after only three.

What have you got in your soil?

As many of the soil-dwellers are so small, we can't see them with the naked eye and so usually have no idea how the soil teems with life. The gardener can get a good idea though from the larger animals he can see. If your soil contains plenty of earthworms, for example, it's a pretty good bet that the smaller organisms will be there too.

Actual numbers vary from place to place, depending on soil type, fertility, organic content, and hence food for the animals and micro-organisms, but the sheer quantity of life in a good soil is astounding. One gram (about 1/30 oz) of fertile soil contains more than one thousand million bacteria, and although fungi can't be counted in the same way, estimates of their size suggest that they're present in similar quantities. No wonder there's a lot of chemical breakdown going on in the soil! It's absolutely riddled with microscopic organisms all busily engaged in chemical activity.

In the upper layers of soil beneath only a square metre (1.2 square yards) of permanent grassland, there are more than 100,000 mites, over 40,000 springtails, several thousand beetles and their larvae, 20 million nematodes, up to 200,000 potworms, several hundred earthworms, and many other animals.

That's quite apart from centipedes, millipedes, woodlice and other small animals in the surface litter. True, some of these are eating other animals or plants, but there

Left, *garden black ants tend aphids on plants and 'milk' them for sugary honeydew by stroking them;* **above**, *the common garden snail comes out into the open after rain;* **below**, *toadstools like these shaggy caps push above ground in the autumn;* **opposite**, *the pearly-white eggs of garden snails and slugs are laid in the soil.*

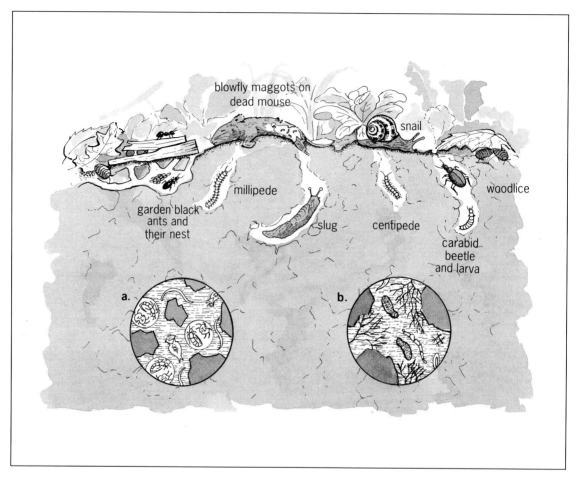

remain teeming thousands of decomposers that fragment and digest dead matter. They'll be at least as plentiful in fertile garden soil where there's lots of organic matter, and they'll all be playing their part in breaking it down so that it's accessible to the bacteria and fungi which can release the nutrients essential to plants.

In other words, the manure and compost that you dig into the soil doesn't feed your plants directly but this happens as a result of the work of the soil animals, bacteria and fungi. It's in your interests to keep the soil in good shape for them so that they will do an absolutely essential job for you.

If you do this, every square centimetre of your top-soil will be the scene of furious

Top, some of the animals and other organisms that live in the soil; left (a), a magnified view of the potworms and nematodes in the water film around soil particles, and the mites and springtails that live in the small air spaces between particles; right (b), a very magnified view of some of the Protozoa, algae, bacteria and fungi that live in the moisture in soil.

activity, much of it on such a microscopic scale that you'll only be aware of it from the good results from your garden plants.

Just imagine it, earthworms and beetles burrow through the soil, while mites and tiny insects roam the air spaces between soil particles, seeking out food. Microscopic Protozoa and aquatic animals swim around in the film of water which coats soil particles, hunting algae, dead organic matter or each other. Nematodes wriggle through moist soil, and tiny potworms and bacteria flourish wherever there's moisture and organic matter they can eat. Around, over and between the soil particles is the filmy, living network of soil fungi. It really is another complete world, living, breathing and working beneath our feet.

RECYCLING OF MATERIALS ESSENTIAL FOR LIFE

The net result of the activities of these millions of soil organisms is the recycling of plant nutrients, so that the chemical elements contained in dead matter eventually become available to our garden plants. Plants manufacture sugars and other organic substances, including starch, cellulose, lignin, fats, pigments, and proteins, but to do this they need many different chemical elements, almost all of which they absorb through their roots.

The one exception to this is carbon, which is a part of all organic compounds and is obtained in the form of carbon dioxide from the atmosphere where it's abundantly available. Abundant though it is, it's not limitless, so its recycling is fundamental to life.

The carbon cycle

The carbon cycle is fairly simple. Green plants absorb carbon dioxide from the air during photosynthesis and use the carbon to make sugars and other organic compounds.

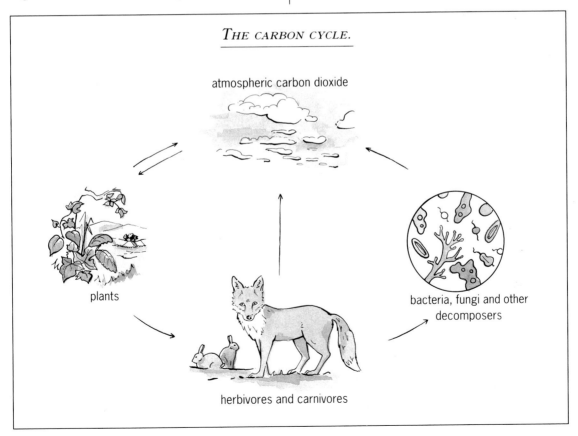

THE CARBON CYCLE.

atmospheric carbon dioxide

plants

herbivores and carnivores

bacteria, fungi and other decomposers

When an animal eats a plant (or another animal, whether alive or dead), the complex organic compounds in its foods are dismantled by the processes of digestion and reassembled to meet its own requirements. Plants, herbivores, carnivores and decomposers all break up sugars to release energy during respiration, and so release carbon dioxide back into the atmosphere.

We take in oxygen for respiration (which takes place in our body cells), when we breathe in, and we breathe out carbon dioxide. So carbon goes round and round from the atmosphere, through plants and animals, and back to the atmosphere.

At certain times, millions of years ago, dead trees and marine animals accumulated without decomposing, forming the fossil fuels, coal and oil. The carbon these trees and animals contained was locked up, eventually to be released as carbon dioxide when coal and oil are burned. There's no stopping the organic cycle.

The calcium cycle

Carbon is an unusual element. Most elements, like calcium for example, never pass into the atmosphere but are taken up in solution through plant roots. Calcium is recycled when it's returned to the soil and to water when animals and plants die and decompose. Plants then absorb the calcium, animals eat the plants or get it from drinking water and so it goes on.

Calcium carbonate is a major component of skeletons and shells, where it may remain

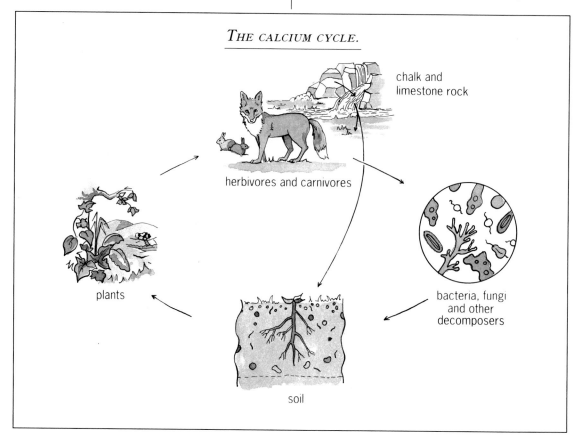

THE CALCIUM CYCLE.

chalk and limestone rock

herbivores and carnivores

bacteria, fungi and other decomposers

plants

soil

locked up after the animal that formed them has died and its soft parts decomposed. Under certain marine conditions in the past, shells accumulated and eventually formed chalk and limestone. Earth movements have raised sea-beds into dry land, where rain and groundwater gradually wear away chalk and limestone, once again releasing calcium.

Other cycles are much more complicated, involving many steps and alternative pathways. One of these, the nitrogen cycle, is of great significance for the gardener: first, because nitrogen is a constituent of all protein and therefore essential for growth; and secondly, because many gardening practices affect its supply and availability. It's worth spending a little time looking in detail at how the nitrogen cycle works.

The nitrogen cycle

Nitrogen is present in abundance as a gas in the atmosphere but plants can only use nitrogen compounds in solution, which they absorb through their roots (usually as nitrates); animals depend on nitrogen compounds, mainly proteins, in their food. There are three routes by which nitrates are formed. First, so-called nitrifying bacteria use ammonia released into the soil when dead plants and animals decompose. Secondly, blue-green algae and nitrogen-fixing bacteria which are abundant in most soils form nitrates from atmospheric nitrogen. And thirdly, to a variable extent nitrates are created by the action of lightning on atmospheric nitrogen.

Not all nitrogen-fixing bacteria live freely in the soil. Many sorts of *Rhizobium* bacteria invade the roots of different legumes like peas and beans, forming characteristic nodules. They take nitrogen from the air and make it available to the plant, so all

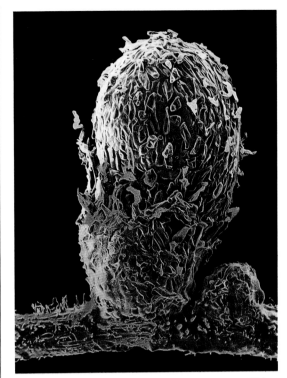

A highly-magnified root nodule on a pea plant. This contains nitrogen-fixing bacteria that convert atmospheric nitrogen to nitrates.

Root nodules on runner bean. All legumes develop nodules and so are important in crop rotation.

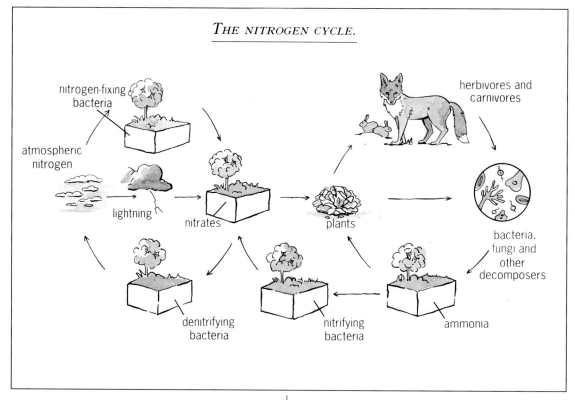

THE NITROGEN CYCLE.

nitrogen-fixing bacteria

atmospheric nitrogen

lightning

nitrates

herbivores and carnivores

plants

bacteria, fungi and other decomposers

denitrifying bacteria

nitrifying bacteria

ammonia

legumes can be grown on soils deficient in nitrogen. Better still, they also enrich the soil around their roots with nitrates which can be used by other plants and this is why they're used in crop rotation schemes.

Alas, there's always a darker side to life which, in the plant world comes in the shape of denitrifying bacteria which use nitrates as a source of energy, releasing nitrogen into the air. Unlike the good guys – the nitrifying bacteria – they don't require oxygen and so thrive in waterlogged soil, which quickly loses its fertility.

LOOKING AFTER YOUR SOIL

If we're intent on doing things nature's way, why do we dig and feed our garden soils when forest and meadow seem to do quite well without it? Well, we expect a much bigger return from our soil in terms of produce than nature ever intended and not just once, but again and again. So we have to keep subsidising the land with energy and nutrients.

Digging is valuable, not just for incorporating manure and compost but also because it creates a deep soil with lots of room for easy root growth. It brings up nutrients from lower levels and improves drainage and aeration on heavy soils.

Deep, double digging in the flower borders is only necessary initially and no more than every ten years or so on the vegetable plot. After that, single digging is all that's required to dig in manure, compost and other fertilisers. Spread these on the surface then incorporate them as you dig, making sure they're distributed through all levels of soil and not just buried at a spade's depth. Breaking up the soil and aerating it makes planting and sowing easier and also benefits

DOUBLE DIGGING.

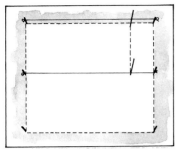

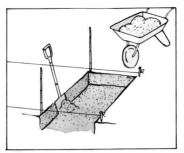

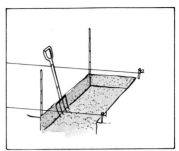

1. Mark out the plot to be dug by setting lines down either side. If it is a wide plot, divide it down the middle as well. Cut two 60 cm (2 ft) canes to mark the width of the trenches. Make each trench exactly the same size.

2. Mark out the first 60 cm (2 ft) trench with the canes and dig out all the soil to the depth of the spade, putting it in a wheelbarrow. Take it to the other end of the plot, so it can be used to refill the last trench.

3. Clean out the crumbs of soil from the bottom of the trench and then 'fork' the soil to the depth of the fork. This is the sub-soil and should not be inverted. Simply loosen it by digging it up and throwing it back as it came out.

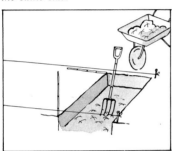

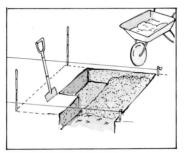

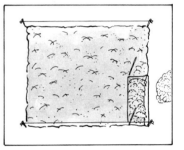

4. Put a 5–8 cm (2–3 in) layer of organic matter in the bottom of the trench. Then, leaving one cane in the corner of the trench you have just dug out, mark out the second trench, to the same size, with the other cane.

5. Start digging out the new trench to the same depth, but throw the soil forwards to cover the organic matter in the first trench. Spread another layer of organic matter in the first trench, cover with remaining soil from the second trench.

6. Carry on working down the plot in this way and, when you get to the last trench, refill it with the soil you removed from the first trench. Cover the entire area with another layer of organic matter. It will soon be washed into the bed by rain.

SINGLE DIGGING.

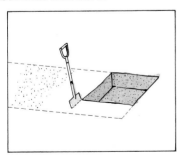

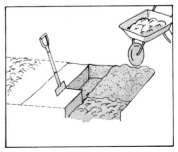

1. Dig out the first trench one spade deep, taking no more than 10 cm (4 in) 'bites'. Throw all the soil behind you, spreading it more or less evenly over the surface of the bed.

2. Spread a layer of manure or compost over the soil about 1 metre (1 yard) behind you; there should be enough to fill up to three trenches with a 5–8 cm (2–3 in) layer of organic matter. Then scrape some forwards into the first trench.

3. Dig a second trench, throwing the soil forwards to cover the organic matter in the first trench. Continue the process until all the organic matter has been dug in. Then spread another layer further down the plot and carry on.

the many oxygen-needing soil bacteria and animals.

Clay soil and silt should be dug in the autumn or when it's moist, although it should be dry enough not to stick to your boots. Both types of soil will benefit by being broken up before the winter frosts so that water has a chance to percolate into the cracks where it will then freeze, forcing clods apart.

The time of digging is not critical for sandy or chalky soils so they're probably best worked over in spring just before you sow or plant.

Crop rotation

As gardeners we make abnormal demands on our soil, however much we feed and pamper it. One way we can balance the demands made on it in the vegetable garden is by crop rotation. Growing one crop year after year in exactly the same place makes quite unreasonable demands on the soil. Different types of plants have different nutritional requirements so by rotating crops we can ensure that the whole spectrum of soil nutrients is tapped.

Most crop rotation schemes incorporate a year under legumes, making the soil more nutritious for subsequent crops.

In the average-sized garden a rotation of three years is ideal. This involves dividing the vegetable garden into three plots, and rotating the cultivation on each of three groups of vegetables. First, the legumes, such as peas and beans, which require no additional nitrogen. Second, the brassicas, such as cabbages, Brussels sprouts and cauliflower (and also turnips and swedes), which have a high demand for nitrogen and benefit from a slightly more limey soil than other vegetables. Third, the root crops, such as carrots, parsnips, beetroot and potatoes.

A SCHEME FOR CROP ROTATION.

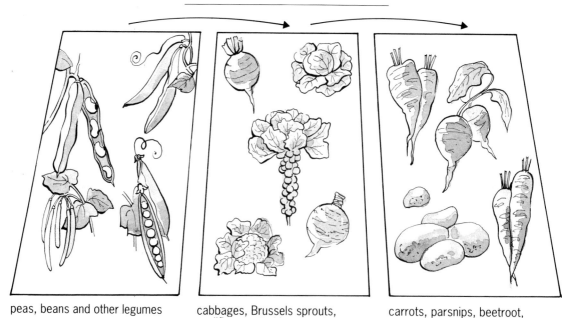

peas, beans and other legumes

cabbages, Brussels sprouts, cauliflowers, turnips, swedes, other brassicas

carrots, parsnips, beetroot, potatoes, other root crops

Conditioning the soil

The best materials to use to condition your soil are well-rotted manure and compost. They improve drainage or water-holding capacity and provide nutrients, although you do need a great deal to boost soil fertility. Some manures, particularly those of pigs or chickens add lots of nitrogen compounds to the soil but little in the way of decaying vegetable matter, so they don't do much to boost the humus content of the soil. Although such manure helps feed the soil, to condition it you do better using manure from herbivores, such as cows, horses and sheep.

Ideally, in the vegetable garden you need two 9-litre (2-gallon) buckets of well-rotted compost or manure for every square metre of soil. The emphasis is on well-rotted because manure with a high straw content, or compost with a lot of fibrous or woody material, has a high carbon content. This means that soil bacteria use the carbon as an energy source and increase so much in numbers that they quickly exhaust the nitrogen compounds and start extracting nitrates from the soil. This is why straw is no good as a soil conditioner if used just before sowing or planting. In the long term, as the bacteria themselves die off and decompose, the nitrogen compounds will be released again but in the short term there's no benefit. And, of course, fresh manure and fresh compost may also contain lots of weed seeds which will cause problems.

Manure and compost can be dug into the soil or used as mulches around trees or shrubs or in the ornamental borders. When using it as a mulch, one bucketful per square metre will usually suffice.

It doesn't matter, as far as nutrients go, whether your source of manure is cows, horses, sheep, pigs or some other animal but if you use chicken manure, be warned, it's very powerful stuff. It's best used as a source of nitrogen for the compost heap or composted in a bin with soaked straw for at least a year. With all manures, you should avoid putting them on young shoots as it'll scorch them.

Many gardeners have access to drifts of fallen tree leaves which they are tempted to add to the compost heap. However, tree leaves contain considerable quantities of lignin, which is slow to rot down, and which is decomposed by fungi rather than bacteria. The best idea is to make two or three separate wire-mesh containers for your dead leaves (because it takes two or three years to make good, crumbly leaf-mould). And when you have it, leaf-mould is almost too good to dig into the soil so you may prefer to use it as a potting or seed-sowing compost.

Dead leaves, particularly any swept from the street, and animal manures may be contaminated with chemical residues of one sort or another, and this is another reason for composting them for a good, long time, so that pollutants wash out.

You'll almost certainly find that you need to feed your soil some additional fertiliser to get the growth and produce you desire. There's no nutritional reason, as far as plants are concerned, why you should use organic rather than inorganic fertilisers – because plants don't distinguish between sources of nitrogen, potassium, phosphorous or whatever.

Organic gardeners, however, are vehement in their claims that organically-grown vegetables taste better. There is also evidence that inorganic, chemical fertilisers disorient earthworms and so make them less effective in working the soil. They find their way to the surface by sensing minute chemical changes and a handful of chemical fertiliser will subject them to a 'chemical storm' and, consequently, they'll not be able to find their way to feed and mate. There's also strong evidence that chemical fertilisers reduce or curtail the activities of soil organisms, so locking up all that free plant food underground.

Blood, fish and bonemeal is a good general compound fertiliser. The thing to watch is that the nitrogen contained in this fertiliser is quickly released, so it should not be spread more than two weeks before crops are sown and planted. Hoof and horn is one of the best sources of slow-release nitrogen, whereas dried blood is very fast-acting. Seaweed meal is even better balanced than blood, fish and bonemeal but is rather expensive. Pelletted chicken manure fertiliser fits the bill very well.

Whatever you choose to use, remember that the organic gardener feeds the soil rather than the plants, resulting in the encouragement of many soil animals, bacteria and fungi, which will end up releasing all the necessary nutrients for your plants.

CHAPTER THREE

COMPOST

It's pretty obvious that a really fertile soil, full of plant food and alive with beneficial organisms, depends on lots of regular applications of bulky organic matter. But where's it going to come from? Not all of us have access to animal manure but one thing we certainly can do is to compost. There's an abundance of material in every garden that can be composted, and more 'fodder' for the heap comes from the kitchen. However small or urban the garden, it's always possible to make compost. Remember that it's one of the best and certainly the cheapest soil conditioner available.

HOW TO MAKE COMPOST

The idea of a compost bin or heap is that in it you concentrate, and often accelerate, the processes of decomposition of dead organic material that normally take place in a more distributed way in the soil. You're aiming to produce as large a quantity as you can of brown, crumbly, sweet-smelling compost, which you can use to condition the soil and to add variable quantities of nutrients.

When dug in or used as a mulch, compost will improve growing conditions for your plants, and your work in preparing and spreading the compost will be rewarded with healthier plants, finer shows of flowers, and more abundant salads, vegetables and herbs for the kitchen.

All this can be achieved without buying in expensive fertilisers and artificial soil conditioners, and, best of all, it's nature's way of doing things. All you're doing is helping along the natural processes.

What to compost

In theory you can compost anything of organic origin but in practice there are a few qualifications. All soft or fairly soft garden waste is ideal: weeds, dead-headed flowers, any vegetation that's clipped back or trimmed, old stems of perennial plants cleared away in autumn, trimmings from harvested vegetables, pea, bean and other plants once they have finished cropping, windfall apples, and so on.

Don't, however, include woody prunings or old cabbage stumps because they'll take too long to rot. They contain large quantities of lignin, which is decomposed by fungi rather than bacteria and fungi operate more slowly. If you want to compost these woody materials, one possible solution is a separate heap in a secluded part of the garden or, better still, use a shredding machine to convert the woody material to chippings for use as a mulch. Shredding machines are a bit expensive but make a great job of converting woody waste into a usable material.

Don't include the roots of persistent weeds in your compost. They will almost certainly continue to grow in the compost container and you'll distribute them around the garden when you spread the compost. This applies particularly to couch grass (*Elymus repens*), ground elder (*Aegopodium podagraria*), hedge bindweed (*Calystegia sepium*), creeping buttercup (*Ranunculus repens*) and large-flowered pink-sorrel (*Oxalis corymbosa*), and you may learn by bitter experience of others. These roots are better burnt or otherwise disposed of.

Any diseased or infected material should also be burnt since it could contaminate the compost and keep the diseases alive to re-infect living plants. This also applies to the top growth of maincrop potatoes, whether it looks diseased or not, because it's usually infected with potato blight spores. It's best not to take any chances with disease and infection.

Also avoid the compost becoming a source of weed seeds, by pulling weeds up and composting them before they set seed. If you miss the boat and they do have seeds, exclude them.

It's often claimed that the heat generated by chemical activity in a compost heap kills seeds and other live material but rarely does it get hot enough to guarantee this, so the best bet is not to take the risk.

Finally, leave out any cooked kitchen scraps which may attract rats and mice. It's not a great loss because they don't compost very well in any case. The easy way round this is to have two waste bins in the kitchen, one destined for the dustbin and the other (with a lid) for vegetable parings, fruit skins, tea leaves, coffee grounds and so on. You'll be amazed how quickly it fills up!

Remember that newspaper and old cotton or woollen clothes are organic too, so these can also go on the heap, although they're best cut into smallish pieces first. But avoid glossy magazines, since the paper doesn't rot down well and contains a high proportion of lead. Obviously, large quantities of paper or cloth may cause problems but some can be used.

Grass cuttings make superb compost but only if they're used properly. If they're put in as a thick layer they'll form a slimy mass and contribute nothing to the compost. The answer with all such short, soft materials is to distribute them through the heap in thin layers. This may mean holding them in reserve by the container until you have enough coarse material to mix with them. You can use larger weeds, shredded newspapers, strawy horse manure or just straw.

The reason for this layering is to ensure that there's enough air around the material to rot it down properly. In the absence of air, the group of bacteria that breaks down nitrates and other compounds to release nitrogen gas, multiplies and starts turning dead vegetation to a stinking slime. Compost containers are always designed so that plenty of air can circulate and to make the

Left, *open compost heaps work quite well but, as the top and sides tend to dry out, need turning regularly to promote the rotting process all through. Such heaps contain much more animal life, such as beetles, centipedes, millipedes and woodlice, than compost containers, and the damper layers are a writhing mass of brandling worms.*

Below, *hedgehogs sometimes visit compost heaps to forage for beetles and other animals to eat. They are one of the few garden animals that eat slugs, as this one is doing, and are a vastly preferable means of slug control to poisonous slug pellets.*

very best compost you'll need to turn it every so often. This is simply a case of throwing it out of the container and putting it back in again, fluffing it up with a fork at the same time to re-aerate it.

What else to add

The bacteria that perform the essential task of decomposing the organic matter in the container need nitrogen themselves to grow and multiply. There's a risk that they'll deplete the nitrogen in the compost and stop growing. So it's usual to add a small amount of nitrogen to compost heaps, ideally in the form of animal manure, or dried blood, seaweed meal or a compost activator bought from a garden shop. Very little is needed, certainly no more than a fine dusting every 30 cm (12 in) of compost. In fact, if your garden is well fed, the plants you're composting will contain enough nitrogen.

Compost heaps tend to become rather acid and that slows down the activity of the all-important bacteria, so it's advisable to add a little lime to neutralise the acidity and keep the compost 'sweet'. Apply a slightly heavier dusting than of nitrogen activator, every 30 cm (12 in) of compost.

An essential ingredient of the compost heap, all too easily forgotten, is water which is needed by the bacteria working on the chemical processes of decomposition. In hot summers, or if you've added dry material such as straw to the heap, you need to water it every so often, so that it stays damp. Don't let it become waterlogged though, or unwelcome bacteria may start breaking down valuable nitrates. You can avoid this during winter, when there's more rain falling, by covering the heap with black polythene sheeting or a piece of old carpet, a strategy that also helps keep up the temperature.

Like all chemical processes, decomposition by bacteria proceeds more rapidly when it's warm. This is why you can make good compost in only two or three months in summer, whereas in winter it's considerably slower. The obvious solution is to prevent heat loss by covering the heap, and for this a piece of old carpet is ideal. It's heavy enough to stay in place but porous enough to 'breathe' and let in air.

Finally, you also need the soil bacteria that do the actual job of decomposition. Luckily, they're present in teeming millions in soil and they multiply rapidly, so there will be enough of them in the soil clinging to the roots of weeds to inoculate the heap. There's no need to add additional soil.

Compost containers

A compost heap can simply be that – a heap of discarded organic material in a secluded corner of the garden. Decomposition will take place in it, and usable compost will be produced. The snag is that the sides and top of the heap tend to dry out, restricting decomposition to the centre and lower levels, so that to be efficient the heap needs turning two or three times during the rotting process, to push unrotted material to the centre.

A partial solution is to make the heap in a pit dug in the ground but there's still a tendency for upper layers to dry out, air circulation is poor which adversely affects the decomposition process, and digging out and using the compost becomes a major, back-breaking exercise.

One attraction of this sort of uncontained heap for the gardener interested in seeing who and what shares his garden is that it'll be obviously and visibly alive with all sorts of animal life: beetles, centipedes, millipedes, woodlice, maybe some tiny but fearsome-looking pseudoscorpions, as well as, in the damper layers, a writhing mass of the reddish earthworms known as brandlings (*Eisenia foetida*). Flies and wasps will visit the heap, and perhaps a hedgehog, foraging for some of the smaller animals to eat. Fascinating to watch, but not the best way to make compost.

To make it efficiently and consistently you need two containers, one that can be left to rot down while the other is filled up. Position them somewhere unobtrusive and ensure that you can easily remove the finished product.

Garden centres sell various sorts of compost containers made of wood or plastic, or it's easy to make them yourself from brick, plastic barrels, chicken wire and posts lined with cardboard, and from wood. In our opinion, wooden containers are ideal, not least because they look good; they're easy to build and can be made so that it's easy to remove the compost.

A wooden compost container (see page 62) is simple to make from old floorboards and floor joists, available from demolition contractors and much cheaper than new timber. The floorboards provide the flat pieces of wood for the box and the removable front panels, and the joists make ideal corner supports. The instructions on page 62 are for making one container, (about 90 cm × 90 cm or 3 ft × 3 ft), but you can easily make a second box alongside, with one side common to both. Note that there are no gaps between the boards. The space at the bottom is quite enough to ensure that air circulates freely whilst retaining maximum heat. When finished the container should stand on a level surface, preferably soil.

Start the heap off with a 15 cm (6 in) layer of coarse material, such as horse manure, straw, or large weeds, to make sure there's a free flow of air at the bottom. Then add more finer material in another layer 15 cm (6 in) deep. You can sprinkle a little compost activator or nitrogen fertiliser over this layer but it shouldn't really be necessary. Best of all, add a shallow layer of horse manure to improve aeration and so that the nitrogen in it acts as the activator. With a fork, mix the layers together a little and then put in another 15 cm (6 in) layer of material plus a dusting of lime. Then put in fine and coarse material as you get it.

Don't forget to cover the container with a piece of carpet or a lid to stop it getting too wet and to cut down on heat loss. The composted materials rot down and shrink quickly so after a few days what seemed like a full container will have room for more.

Each container should give you two good binfuls during the summer, one early on, the other in late autumn, and then there should be another formed over winter and ready in the spring.

The quality of the compost you get out of the bins will vary depending on the nature and quality of the organic material you put in. From a large heap using only the best materials, properly treated, you'll get brown, crumbly, sweet-smelling compost. The more usual experience is that compost contains a lot of semi-rotted, fibrous material, and is variable in quality. Don't be afraid to use it though, because it'll still improve the soil and certainly do no harm, even though it takes rather longer to become humus.

WHAT HAPPENS IN THE COMPOST HEAP

A carefully made compost heap in a container will not be occupied by anything like the variety of the larger, more visible animals you can see in a more casually constructed, unenclosed compost heap.

Left, *brandling worms abound in compost heaps and containers where they eat the rotting organic material and excrete finely-divided matter and mucus as wormcasts. They get into compost because their eggs are in the soil clinging to weed roots.*

Right, *very highly magnified bacterium of the sort that lives in well-aerated soil. The whip-like 'tails' or* flagellae *enable it to move through the water film on soil particles. The colours are false, resulting from the photographic method.*

Below, *double digging to make a deep-bed. Quantities of compost are incorporated as the bed is dug to two spades' depth, providing lots of room for root growth. Once it is made, work from the sides – never walk on a deep-bed, as this would compact it.*

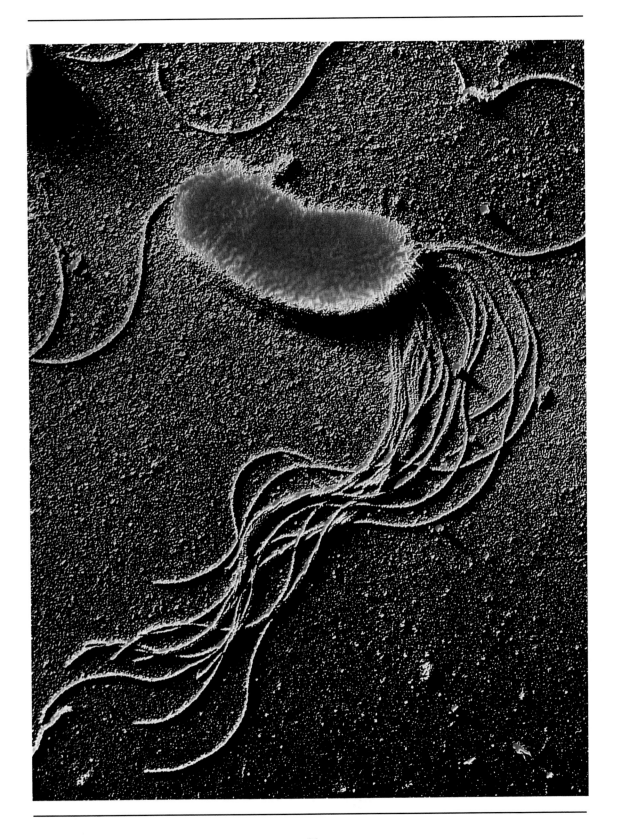

You can make your container whatever size suits the space you have, varying the length of the wood for the sides and front panel to make different sized containers. You will need:

4 pieces of 5 × 10 cm (2 × 4 in) wood, each 1 m (3 ft) long – for the uprights
19 pieces of wood, each 1 m (3 ft) long – 18 for the sides and 1 for the front
5 pieces of wood, each 75 cm (2 ft 6 in) long – to make the front panels
4 battens, each 75 cm (2 ft 6 in) long
2 small pieces of wood – to secure the battens
1 piece of wood, 1 cm (½ in) thick – to use as a spacer
strong galvanised nails

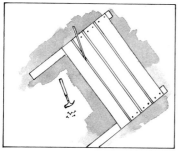

1. Make the first side. Lay two uprights on the ground 75 cm (2 ft 6 in) apart. Starting about 7.5 cm (3 in) from the bottom, lay six side planks across them at 90° angle, using the spacer to make gaps between them. Nail them securely on to the uprights. Repeat the process to make a second side.

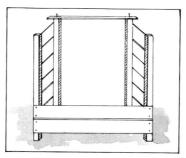

2. Make the back. Hold both sides upright, about 1 m (3 ft) apart and tack a piece of wood across to hold in place while you nail on six pieces to form the back. Start near the bottom and make each piece level with those on the sides, so space is allowed for ventilation.

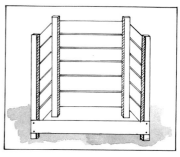

3. Start to make the front. Nail a 1 m (3 ft) board across the front of the uprights 7.5 cm (3 in) from the bottom.

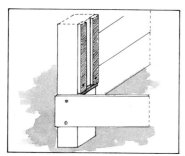

4. Nail four battens on to the front uprights as shown. Check there is enough room between them to allow you to slide in the front panels. To stop these panels sliding out when you fill the container, nail a piece of wood across the bottom of each side.

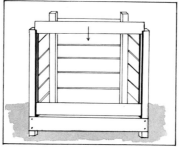

5. One by one, slide all the front panels in between the battens. If they are too long you may need to cut them to fit.

6. Using a water-based wood preservative, paint the whole container thoroughly and leave it to dry. Slide the front panels back into the container. To stop the sides bulging when you fill it, tie string across the top.

This doesn't matter at all. The smaller animals and particularly the all-important bacteria are there in their millions, doing the essential job of decomposing all the organic matter you pile in.

The hotter the heap becomes, the more animal life will be excluded, but not the essential bacteria, which will work better and multiply more rapidly the warmer it gets.

In a casually constructed, open compost heap, organic material in the upper, drier and coolest layer is chewed, eaten, partially digested, and otherwise fragmented by such small animals as woodlice and perhaps also by millipedes, although these are not usually abundant.

Beetles and centipedes scavenge and hunt through the litter, and fly larvae feed in the damper places. Mites and tiny insects such as springtails also work on the material, using it as food. The waste products, the sloughed skins and the dead bodies of all these animals contribute to the organic melting pot of the heap into which they slowly sink.

In the lower, damper levels are hundreds of thousands of potworms and brandling worms, which use this fragmented organic material as food, breaking it down even further. The dead bodies of these animals, their faeces, the much-divided and fragmented remains of the organic material originally piled on the heap, are all eventually digested and decomposed by bacteria and to a lesser extent by fungi.

In other words, what goes on in the casually constructed compost heap is much the same as decomposition in the soil, with the same animals and micro-organisms playing their part – it's just happening in a far more concentrated way and at a faster rate.

If, however, you make a carefully constructed heap in a closed container, paying attention to aeration, moisture, and the provision of nitrogen and lime, the compost-making process will be even faster and more consistent.

There may be fewer, if any, of the larger animals, such as woodlice, that contribute to the initial breaking up of the raw organic material in an open heap, but the temperature will rise and stay much higher. The main contributors to decomposition will be bacteria.

When you shred and mix the material to put into the heap, you do much of the work done in the soil by the larger soil animals, and ensure that the organic matter is in a form that's accessible to bacteria and other micro-organisms. Careful, layered construction of the heap means that bacteria are working all through it on the end stages of decomposition that release nitrates, sulphates and so on into the compost.

Fungi are less numerous in such a carefully maintained compost heap than in the soil but they're still active, and when the resulting compost is spread over or dug into the soil, fungi will continue to work on it there, completing the humification process.

Brandling worms are usually very numerous in a casually constructed heap but sometimes less so in a bacteria-oriented heap. However, they're very valuable because they eat and digest organic material. Like earthworms, they work and mix the material in which they live and feed and improve its structure by excreting finely-divided material coated with mucus. This all makes organic matter much more accessible to bacteria and other micro-organisms and the processes of decomposition are accelerated.

For this reason, some gardeners like to

A double wooden compost bin. This is two containers of the sort illustrated on page 62, with one side common to both. One container is left to rot while the other is filled.

add brandling worms to their compost heaps. They can be bought from fishing-tackle shops, where they're sometimes known as 'tiger worms', or you may be able to delve through a friend's compost or manure heap where you'll certainly find lots of them. Even if you don't add them specially, you'll generally find them in the heap after a while. They come originally from eggs in the soil added to the heap attached to weed roots. They don't live long in soil and are never numerous but really do well in compost heaps because of the abundance of food and the elevated temperature.

HOW TO USE COMPOST

Once the heap has done its job and you have a supply of compost, whether it's the brown, crumbly ideal or a more fibrous mixture, you must put it to good use in the garden. The aim is to incorporate it in the soil to improve its structure, accelerate the formation of humus and, to a variable extent, to boost nutrient levels.

An increasingly popular and very rewarding procedure is to make deep-beds, particularly for growing vegetables, although it also helps for ornamentals. The plants are grown in narrow beds, no more

Above, Lithobius forficatus, *the commonest garden centipede, is predatory on other small soil animals.*

Below, *the pill-bug, a woodlouse present in most gardens but more abundant on chalky soil.*

Digging a deep-bed.

It is essential that the soil is loose and dug deeply and that it is enriched with plenty of organic matter. Never tread on the bed once it has been dug, as this compacts the soil.

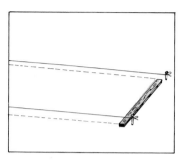

1. Mark one edge of the bed with a planting line. Measure 1.25 m (4 ft) across using a planting board and set up another planting line parallel to the first.

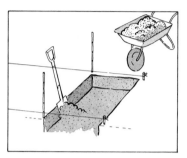

2. Using canes, mark a trench 60 cm (2 ft) wide. Dig out the trench one spade deep, put the soil in a wheelbarrow and take it to the other end of the bed; it is used to fill the last trench.

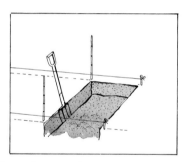

3. Break up the exposed sub-soil in the bottom of the trench with a fork. This enables the roots to penetrate more deeply.

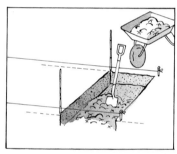

4. Put a 5–8 cm (2–3 in) layer of well-rotted manure or compost into the bottom of the trench. This enriches the soil and improves its texture.

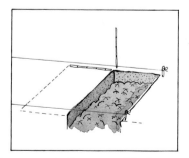

5. Leaving a cane in the corner of the first trench, measure the second 60 cm (2 ft) section with the other cane. Making all the trenches the same size ensures that they contain the same amount of soil.

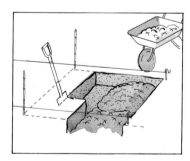

6. Start digging the soil from the second trench and transfer it into the first trench, spreading it out to cover the organic matter.

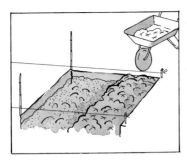

7. *Put another 5–8 cm (2–3 in) layer of manure/compost into the first trench. Because of the bulk of the added organic matter, the bed will be raised as you work.*

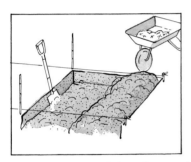

8. *Continue to dig out the soil from the second trench and cover the new layer of manure/compost. This leaves a deep-bed of loose, organically enriched soil in the first trench.*

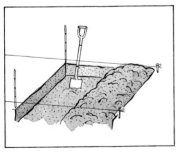

9. *Scrape all the soil from the bottom of the second trench and break up the exposed soil. Repeat steps 4– 8 and use the soil taken to the end of the plot to cover the manure/compost in the final trench.*

than 1.25 m (4 ft) wide, and of whatever length is convenient, with access paths in between. Initially, dig the bed deeply, to two spades' depth and incorporate quantities of compost, providing lots of room for easy root growth. After this never walk on the bed as this would risk compacting it but work instead from the sides. If you absolutely must get on to the bed, use boards or planks to stand on so that your weight is distributed. After the initial deep digging, you can incorporate more compost by single digging – remembering not to walk on the bed. Because plant roots can penetrate deeply into the worked and loosened soil, competition between them is lessened and you can plant more densely, more than doubling the yield per square metre.

If you don't want to make deep-beds, the best way of using your compost is to dig it into the top layers of the soil but it can also be used as a mulch around vegetables and ornamentals. If the soil is moist when you put it on the mulch will keep it moist, suppress weeds, and gradually become incorporated with the soil. Don't, however, be misled into thinking that this is an easy option and an alternative to digging in compost. The more you can incorporate into your soil the better.

Just a word of warning. If the compost is not well-rotted, it'll tend to make the soil rather acid, as acid substances are produced in the early stages of decay. Also, much carbon dioxide is produced by the many animals and bacteria that are involved in the initial stages of decomposition, and this together with the increased acidity may damage plant roots.

If you dig no organic material at all into your soil, you risk losing soil structure as crumb formation is not encouraged and, of course, humus formation stops. Eventually,

the soil humus will be depleted, with further loss of soil structure and a reduction in the release of nutrients in forms plants can use. Your soil will become dead and lifeless and it will be almost useless as a growing medium.

The addition of chemical fertilisers instead of organic matter will also do nothing for soil structure. Although nutrients are added in a usable form, this flush of food is no substitute for the continual, slow release by soil organisms which ensures that nutrients are always present when a plant needs them.

The deep, loose, well-aerated, enriched soil of a deep-bed allows closer planting than would otherwise be the case, yet vegetables and ornamentals flourish and look attractive planted together. Yields are dramatically increased by using deep-beds.

What's more, heavy applications of chemical fertilisers make the valuable worms and micro-organisms in the soil less effective.

There's no substitute for well-made garden compost or well-composted manure for improving and conditioning the soil. They don't contain as high a proportion of nutrients as is sometimes supposed but they certainly add something nutritious. And the teeming hordes of soil animals and bacteria, implementing the recycling of nutrients (see page 25), will do the rest for you.

CHAPTER FOUR

SEEDS AND HOW THEY GROW

Every gardener who's ever put a seed in the soil will know the delicious agony of anticipation that follows sowing and the tingle of excitement when the first green shoots appear. What's more, it never leaves you. However long you've been gardening, however many successful seasons you've had, you'll still have the same old self-doubt when you sow and the same glow of pleasure when germination begins.

Mind you, not every sowing effort is successful, for a variety of reasons, but fortunately gardeners are, in the main, philosophers. When that carefully nurtured patch of seeds fails to appear the first feeling of disappointment is quickly replaced by a shrug of the shoulders in the sure knowledge that you can have another go next year. Things are *always* better then!

Still, it does seem a bit unfair when all nature does is to scatter the seed on the ground in one way or another and, as if by magic, they germinate. Well, if you feel that, console yourself with the knowledge that in fact nature sows hundreds, possibly thousands of seeds from one plant, out of which only a tiny proportion actually germinates. That's a major part of most plants' survival mechanism.

None the less, despite that seemingly low success rate, plants have developed often quite extraordinarily sophisticated methods of ensuring that the maximum number of seeds develop and that, when they do, they stand the best chance of survival.

If we gardeners understand those methods we stand a very much better chance of success.

WHAT SEEDS NEED FOR GERMINATION

Provided seeds are kept cool and dry in their packets as is recommended, they won't germinate. Obviously they need different conditions for growth and the three essentials are water, air (to be accurate, oxygen) and a varying degree of warmth.

Water is necessary first of all because the swelling caused by taking it up ruptures the tough, protective seed-coat and allows the germination process to start. After that there's furious chemical activity associated with growth, all of which requires water. A broad bean seed, for instance, takes on one and a half times its original weight of water prior to germination, and goes on using it at a rapid rate.

Oxygen is needed because once the embryonic plant within the seed starts to grow and develop, its tissues are actively and busily working, liberating the energy that powers all that's going on.

A certain amount of warmth is needed because all chemical reactions – and there are many going on in a germinating seed – occur faster at higher temperatures. The amount of heat needed depends on what the plant is used to under natural conditions. French marigolds (*Tagetes patula*) from Mexico, for example, need at least 18°C (64°F), while the European viper's bugloss (*Echium plantagineum*) germinates outside in the spring when the soil temperature reaches 7°C (45°F).

SEED DORMANCY

The seeds of almost all plants are in a dormant state. Growth stops and their metabolism is slowed to a rate only just enough to keep them alive. This 'hibernation' is vital to get them through winter cold or summer drought and to survive the rigours of their dispersal systems.

To ensure they don't compete with each other or with the parent plant, they may be carried great distances by wind or water, snagged to the fur of an animal or even inside it. Through all these difficult and hazardous times, they're protected by their hard seed-coat. And an excellent protector it generally proves to be.

The oldest living seeds ever discovered were 1,000-year-old lotus seeds, found embedded in peat on the site of an ancient lake in Manchuria. They have exceedingly hard coats which have to be broken down before germination can start and, when they were broken 1,000 years after being distributed, every one germinated.

Some seeds are remarkably resistant to heat and extreme cold. Seeds in raspberry jam, which were boiled in the making, have been sown and successfully germinated while others have survived immersion in liquid nitrogen at −250°C. They'll put up with some quite extreme conditions but nevertheless it's still advisable to store yours in the cool, dry conditions recommended.

There are many different ways that seed dormancy is achieved, depending on the particular plant. It could be a reduction of oxygen, drying out, the presence of chemicals which specifically inhibit germination, or just the hardness of the seed-coat.

The important thing for gardeners to recognise is that species differ greatly. Many need a relatively long dormant period but some, like willows, love-in-a-mist and teasels, will germinate almost immediately they're formed. Seeds of teasel will often germinate while still in the seed-head on the parent plant, while willows lose their ability to grow after only about a week. Indeed, several perennials in particular need to be sown when the seed is freshly harvested from the plant. The longer it's left, the lower are your chances of success.

As a very general rule of thumb, most annuals are best sown in the spring but most perennials should be sown as soon after collection as possible.

Most seeds will germinate quite rapidly after being given optimum conditions of moisture, air and warmth. But some need a

quite specific jolt to get them going. The reason is to give the young seedlings the optimum chance of survival after germination and thus ensure the perpetuation of the species.

Lettuces, for example, originated in the near East, where summers are very hot. So they're equipped with a mechanism that prevents them germinating at temperatures above 20°C (68°F) which is too hot for the young seedlings to survive. If you've been sowing your early lettuce in the greenhouse at higher temperatures, that's the reason for your disappointing results. In fact, even outside, in a hot summer, soil temperatures can rise above this so sowing in a shady spot is the order of the day.

Many seeds of trees and shrubs from temperate areas and most alpines need a period of cold before they'll start to grow. This ensures that they lie dormant through the winter and germinate only when the worst of the cold weather is past. Gardeners use this knowledge by sowing early in the year and leaving the containers outside or in a ventilated cold frame to experience the worst of the winter weather unprotected. Alternatively, you can achieve the same effect by putting the seeds in the freezer for a week or two. It seems hard-hearted somehow but it generally results in a good showing of green shoots in the spring. Some plants flower earlier or will only flower if the seeds from which they grow were subjected to the cold treatment. This is known as vernalisation.

*Above left, viper's bugloss Echium plantagineum germinates in spring when the soil temperature reaches 7°C (45°F); **above right**, seeds of teazel will often germinate while still in the seed-head; **left**, French marigolds Tagetes patula germinate when soil temperatures reach 18°C (65°F).*

Other seed-coats are so tough that they need to decay or be broken open before germination can proceed. They'll eventually soften and break down in damp soil or compost but germination of something like *Convolvulus minor* can be hastened if the seeds are rubbed down between two sheets of sandpaper. Obviously you have to go carefully to avoid damaging the enclosed embryo.

A really graphic example of the effect of environment on the evolution of plants is that the seeds of many plants native to Australian deserts and scrubland can only germinate after their seed-coats have been destroyed by one of the regular bushfires. So, they germinate after, rather than before the fire – and survive.

Many hard seeds in fruits are normally softened to some extent by their passage through the guts of animals that eat the fruit, their digestive enzymes weakening the seed-coats. If you have an Oregon grape (*Mahonia aquifolium*) you may have noticed that, though seedlings grow wherever a blackbird has defecated the seed, those that have simply fallen on the ground beneath the bush fail to germinate.

In Mauritius, botanists were puzzled that the few surviving tambalocoque trees were all more than 300 years old. The trees produced apparently fertile seed enclosed in a thick, hard seed-coat but they failed to germinate. Then the fruits were fed to captive turkeys, which have muscular stone-filled gizzards that grind and crush seed-coats. What came out of the other end was viable seed. The only bird on Mauritius that could have achieved the same feat was the dodo – which became extinct about 300 years ago.

The seed-coats of some seeds contain chemical germination inhibitors which, under natural conditions, are slowly soaked out and washed away. Presumably these inhibitors serve to prevent seedlings germinating beneath or close to the parent plant. Spinach and beetroot seed-coats include such germination inhibitors and this is why spinach and beetroot seeds germinate better and more quickly if they're thoroughly washed, or soaked overnight in water, before sowing.

A trick that's effective in germinating many 'reluctant' seeds, such as parsnip which takes so long to come through that it may rot in the soil, or lettuce which will not germinate if it's too warm, is to get them started before sowing. Seeds like lettuce or parsnip can be sprinkled on to damp blotting paper or tissues in a plastic sandwich-box and put in a warmish place until they germinate. Don't forget them because you need to sow them as soon as the developing root has pushed out of the ruptured seed-coat and is about 3 mm ($\frac{1}{8}$ in) long. Large seeds can then be picked out carefully, using blunt tweezers, and appropriately placed in a seed-drill in the soil.

Small seeds are more safely and efficiently sown in a jelly. Make it with a proprietary brand of alginate gel bought from a garden centre, or with wallpaper paste that contains no fungicide. Gently mix in the germinated seeds, and put the mixture into a polythene bag. Cut a hole in one corner and squeeze it carefully into the seed-drill. Water before and after sowing, and make sure you keep it moist and the seedlings will be up in a flash.

How seeds germinate

There are basically two types of seed. Some have food stores within the seed leaves (or cotyledons), which are thick and fleshy, and others have thin cotyledons and a separate

PRE-GERMINATION OF SEEDS AND SOWING THEM IN A JELLY.

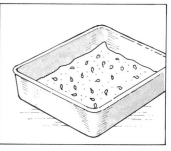

1. Sprinkle such 'difficult' seeds as lettuce or parsnip on to damp blotting paper or tissues in a plastic sandwich box and place somewhere fairly warm.

2. As soon as a developing root shows on the seeds, stir them gently into a jelly made from alginate gel bought from a garden centre or wallpaper paste that contains no fungicide.

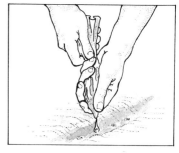

3. Put the mixture into a polythene bag, cut a hole in one corner and carefully squeeze the seed mixture into a prepared seed-drill. Water the drill both before and after sowing, and keep it moist.

store of food within the seed-coat. If you cut open a broad bean lengthwise, you'll find a tiny embryonic plant lying between the fleshy cotyledons to which it's attached. On one side is a minute shoot, and on the other side a tiny root.

Most of the plants we grow have two seed leaves and are known as dicotyledons, but a few, like grass, lilies and onions, have only one seed leaf and they're called monocotyledons.

When a seed like a broad bean, which has its food stores in the cotyledons, germinates, the young shoot grows quickly, pushing its way above the soil where the leaves unfurl. The cotyledons stay below the soil surface and for a while they function as a food reservoir.

On the other hand, when germination takes place in a seed like a sunflower which has thin cotyledons and a separate food store, things happen the other way around. The root grows rapidly, pushing the seed leaves up into the air where they quickly turn green and start making food from sunlight by photosynthesis. Often the split seed-coat stays stuck to the seed leaves for a while and continues to provide stored food.

The stored food in a seed is used to provide the energy and nutrients for germination and early growth. Obviously, there must be enough in the reserves to allow the seedling at least to break through the surface, so it's easy to see the dangers of sowing too deeply. The smaller the seed, the smaller the food reserves so the shallower it should be sown. Indeed, there's little doubt that the biggest single cause of failure of seeds to germinate is sowing too deeply.

Water is absolutely essential to start the germination process going. Not only does it swell up the tissues inside the seed and so break the seed-coat but it also activates enzymes. These substances convert the stored food into soluble nutrients which can then be transported to the growing tips. For germination to be successful, those nutrients must be made available pretty fast.

In some seeds, like celery and busy lizzies, the enzymes are activated by light so it's essential not to exclude it by covering with a deep layer of compost or by putting a piece of black polythene over the seed tray. Small seeds don't need covering at all but if larger ones need a bit to retain moisture, use vermiculite which will do this and still let light through.

Whichever way up you sow a seed, the shoot will always grow up and the root down. So it doesn't matter at all how the seed lands when it hits the soil. For gardeners that's just as well!

This very convenient trick is simply a response to gravity, and it's quite easy to demonstrate it for yourself. If you get a seed growing, perhaps in a jamjar, and then rotate it so that the direction of gravitational pull is constantly changing, both the shoot and the root will assume corkscrew shapes.

This is the result of the accumulation under gravity of a plant growth substance known as an 'auxin', which is produced in the tip of the shoot and percolates down through the rest of the plant. When it accumulates on one side of a shoot, it causes extra growth on that side, resulting in an upwards bend. When it accumulates on one side of a root, growth is slowed on that side, resulting in a downwards bend. So shoots always grow away from the pull of gravity while roots grow towards it. If the tip of the shoot growing from a germinating seed is damaged or removed, growth will stop in shoot and root.

Opposite, *a colourful alpine garden growing on a raised bed. One-third of the depth of a raised bed should be of coarse drainage (such as broken bricks) and the soil mixture used for growing alpines should include considerable quantities of grit.*

Above, *the berries of* Mahonia *are eaten by blackbirds which defecate the seeds. These seeds, softened by digestive processes, soon germinate and grow well, whereas the hard seed-coat inhibits germination of seeds taken straight from the berries.*

PUTTING IT INTO PRACTICE

Armed with the knowledge of how germination works best, it's much easier to achieve ideal conditions in the garden. And that, of course, means a much higher success rate.

The simplest and certainly the cheapest way is to sow directly in the soil outside but there's little point in starting too early. The seed packet will give you a good indication of when to start. Different plants need different temperatures but there's rarely any point in sowing anything until the soil temperature reaches about 7°C (45°F) except, of course, those plants that need a cold spell to trigger germination.

If you want to be really scientific you can invest in a soil thermometer but after a while experience will tell you when to get sowing. In the good old days, farmers would walk into the middle of a field, drop their trousers and sit on the soil bare-bottomed for a really sensitive reading but that's perhaps carrying things a bit too far!

For a really early start, warm up the soil with a cloche or simply by covering it with a sheet of clear polythene.

Having established the optimum temperature, the next essential is water and this will depend greatly on good preparation.

Ideally, the soil will have been dug over with some form of bulky organic matter worked in to help hold water and nutrients and to supply a home for those countless millions of soil organisms.

Then rake it down roughly and, if it's at all spongy, consolidate it by treading all over it, shuffling along with your weight on your heels. Then rake it down finally to make a fine, crumbly tilth.

Finely raked but firmed down soil holds the seeds more securely so that when the fragile young root emerges from the seed it's immediately in contact with the soil particles and in a position to absorb water and nutrients. If the individual soil particles are close together, water is held in a film around them and is pulled towards the seeds as they take up the water.

Although the soil should be firm, it mustn't be set like concrete or the young shoot will have difficulty getting out. So, after sowing, cover with a little soil and just tap down gently with the back of the rake. And never water after sowing since this could cause a crust to form on the top of the soil, again preventing emergence. If the soil's dry, water down the drill *before* sowing and then cover with dry soil.

When you do sow, remember that the seeds' food store is quite small, so don't give the seedlings a hard time by putting the seeds too deep. The instructions will often recommend a 6 mm ($\frac{1}{4}$ in) drill but of course that's quite impossible to measure. Just make it as shallow as you can, using a draw hoe or, easier still, a stick. But obviously, larger seeds can and should go in more deeply.

Seeds are normally sown in straight rows though that's not always necessary. It doesn't happen in nature after all. But this is another example of the way our intelligence can give us the edge. Even if you want to sow a round patch of seed in the flower border, for example, it's best to sow in rows because that way you can distinguish the seeds you've sown from the weeds that nature's contributed. Yours are the ones in straight lines and the rest can be pulled out.

Spacing depends on the size and type of plant and there will always be a recommendation on the seed packet. In general, the larger the seeds the more widely they need to be spaced. Remember that all the plants will be in competition with each other for food, water and light, so space them so that it's shared out equally and all your plants will benefit.

There's another way too that you can keep one jump ahead of the weeds. Before you prepare the seed-bed allow the weed seeds to germinate freely. Then, just before you rake down for sowing, hoe them all off. It's an old gardeners' trick called the 'stale seed-bed' and it ensures that at least the first batch of weed seedlings are defeated before you sow and that your seeds will have a head start.

Whatever you're growing, sow thinly. Most seeds these days will have a pretty high germination rate and naturally those seedlings you have to pull out and throw away to give space to those remaining are wasted. Some can be transplanted but by no means all.

But however thinly you sow, the seedlings will be overcrowded when they come up so some thinning will be necessary. Water the row of seedlings the day before thinning, to minimise root damage, and remove the unwanted seedlings carefully. With two

PREPARING A SEED-BED IN THE GARDEN AND SOWING SEEDS.

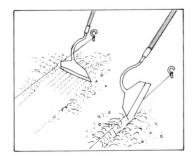

1. Having roughly raked over a bed of good, deep soil containing plenty of organic matter, consolidate it by shuffling along on your heels.

2. Having sprinkled some fertiliser, such as seaweed meal, rake the bed down to a fine tilth.

3. Depending on the size and type of seed, make wide or narrow shallow drills by dragging along the edge or the corner of the hoe.

4. Water along the drills with the fine rose of a watering can.

PREPARATION OF A SEED-BED
(CONTINUED).

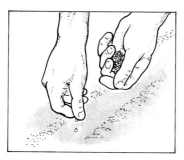

5. Sprinkle or place the seeds in the watered drill. The larger the seeds, the more widely they need to be spaced. Be guided by the instructions on the seed packet.

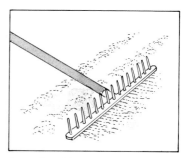

6. Cover the seeds with a thin layer of dry soil pulled into the drill using the back of a rake.

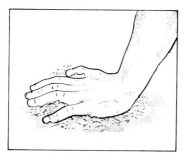

7. Firm down the soil over the seeds using your hands. This will ensure they are in contact with the damp soil.

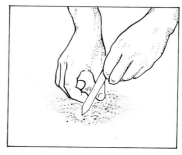

8. Always label the row so that you know what you've planted and where.

fingers, hold the soil firm around the seedlings you wish to keep. If the thinned seedlings are not needed, put them immediately on the compost heap, to avoid the bruised stems attracting pests and diseases. If you need the thinnings for additional planting, lift them very carefully with a dibber or a small trowel, so that the roots remain intact, and lay them temporarily in a seed tray.

Transplant the seedlings carefully to their new positions, holding them by their leaves rather than their stems. The tender stems bruise easily and soon attract slugs and other pests and diseases. Firm down the transplanted seedlings so that they're well settled, and water them in.

Most seedlings can be successfully transplanted but root crops are not suitable for transplanting as they tend to 'fork'.

SOWING UNDER COVER

As you would expect, some plants from warmer climates need extra heat for germination and early growth. A heated greenhouse, a propagator or even the airing cupboard coupled with a warm, sunny windowsill can get them started earlier.

Left, *when a broad bean germinates, the fleshy cotyledons stay beneath the soil and serve as a food reservoir. The young shoot quickly elongates and pushes above the soil surface, where the leaves unfurl and start manufacturing sugars.*

Below, *germination of clover seeds, showing the development of numerous root hairs from the main root. What appear to be leaves are the cotyledons, which provide the young seedling with food until the leaves appear. The dark brown husks half-way up the stems are the split and shed seed-coats.*

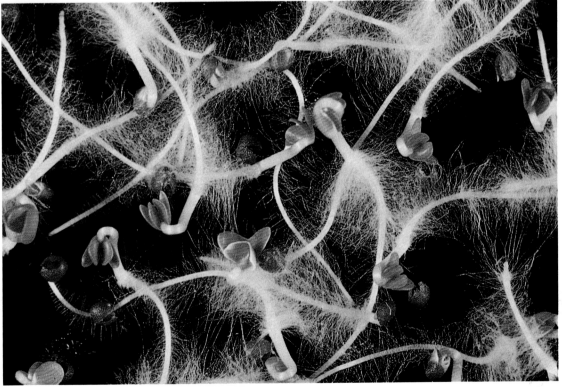

You can also start hardier plants like cabbage and lettuce indoors to get them earlier. Some gardeners have such slug problems that they start everything in the greenhouse where they have more control early on.

Growing in containers can't be considered natural so you have to take special steps to compensate. It's folly, for example, to expect garden soil, which grows perfectly good plants outside, to perform in pots. It won't, so make sure you use a proper seed compost.

Seed compost is expensive and the temptation is always to eke it out by mixing it with garden-quality peat. But peat contains no nutrients so this may be a false economy as you'll have to start feeding the germinated seedlings almost immediately. Seed compost is made using either a peat base or a loam base. Some gardeners prefer to use one, some the other. Peat-based compost is easier to work with but tends to dry out more rapidly and, once dry, is hard to wet again. The best course is to ensure that it's thoroughly moist before using it. This may mean hand-mixing a pile of it with water on the greenhouse bench – rather like mixing bread dough.

There are justifiable concerns about using peat and peat-based products in the garden because of the very real threat to our diminishing areas of peat in wetlands such as the Somerset Levels. Commercial extraction, mainly to make garden products, is putting at risk vulnerable and endangered communities of plants and animals. A recently-developed alternative to peat as a base for compost is fibrous coir derived from waste coconut husks. Coir-based composts are fibrous and a little trickier to use than the traditional material but they give excellent seed germination. It's important to avoid overwatering them

and to start liquid feeding after about three weeks – a little earlier than peat-based composts.

Once the seeds are in place, cover with their own depth of vermiculite or a sprinkling of seed compost from a sieve, depending on whether they need light for germination. Very small seeds, however, don't need any covering, and don't forget to put labels in the trays or pots – you won't remember what everything is!

SOWING SEEDS IN TRAYS OR POTS.

1. Fill seed trays right to the top with good quality compost.

2. Level off with a levelling board or the flat blade of a knife.

3. Water the compost using the fine rose on a watering can.

4. Make two equally-spaced shallow grooves (drills) in the compost, and trickle in a thin row of seeds from your hand or the packet. Larger seeds need to be more widely spaced.

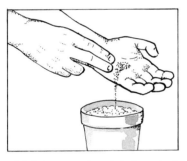

5. Fine seed is better sown in a pot of compost prepared as in steps 1, 2 amd 3. To spread the seed more evenly, first mix it with the same amount of silver sand.

6. Cover the seed with a thin sprinkling of compost from a sieve, or with vermiculite.

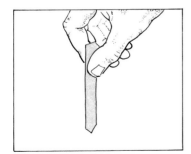

7. Label all the pots and trays of seed. With many flowers, it's also a good idea to put the colour on the label.

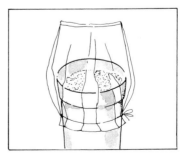

8. To stop the compost drying out, cover with polythene (black for those that need darkness to germinate, clear for those that need light). Remove the polythene as soon as the first seedling appears.

If you use modular polystyrene containers for seed-sowing, a handy practice that saves time later on is what is known as multiple sowing. Small pinches of flower seed or several vegetable seeds can be sown in each module and all left there even when they germinate. When it comes to planting out, the entire block of plants is transplanted together, producing a clump of plants. This is particularly effective with hardy annuals but also works with other flowers. It even works for such vegetables as onions, for the growing plants 'elbow' each other aside and make their own space, but this method cannot be used for long-root crops, such as carrots and parsnips, whose roots become entwined and distorted.

Once you've sown the seeds try to provide the same conditions the seeds would expect in their natural habitat. Again, firm the compost to put the young roots in direct contact when they emerge but don't overfirm so that you drive out the necessary air.

Provide moisture by watering the compost *before* sowing or you may wash the seeds into patches or even right out of the container! And give the correct amount of heat by putting the containers into a propagator. But again, don't overdo it – remember those lettuces that won't germinate in temperatures over 20°C (68°F).

The same rules apply to spacing too. Sow as thinly as you can, even mixing fine seed such as lobelia or snapdragon with a little silver sand to distribute it more evenly. That ensures that each seedling will have enough food and water until the time it's removed and transplanted to fresh compost.

It's a good idea in the greenhouse to retain a little humidity and stop the top of the compost drying out. For seeds that need dark cover with black polythene or glass covered with paper, and for light-lovers use

MULTIPLE SOWING IN MODULES

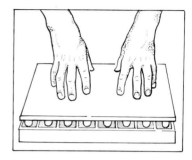

1. Fill the compartments of the modular block with compost and firm down, using the pegged board provided. Water well using a fine rose on the watering can.

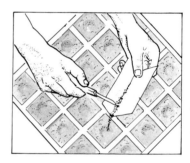

2. Sprinkle about half a dozen seeds into each depression caused by the firming process. As they grow, they will 'elbow' each other aside.

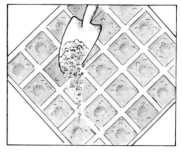

3. Scatter a layer of compost from a trowel on to each group of seeds and lightly water again. When ready for transplanting, move each little block of plants together.

When thinning seedlings, firm soil around those remaining in the soil. These are radishes.

Annual bedding plants. When plants are well grown and compact, harden off before planting out.

Lettuces and courgettes hardening off in cold frame. Ventilate the frame a little more each day.

a clear material. Both must be removed as soon as the first seedling appears.

Once the seedlings are big enough to handle they're transferred to wider spacings in larger containers and this is done in much the same way as transplanting outside. Handle by the leaves, lever the seedlings out carefully with a piece of stick and drop them into the holes in the new compost. Then firm and water and they'll grow away as if they've never been moved.

Having persuaded these gullible seedlings that they're in their native country, perhaps Mexico or South Africa, you need to break the news very gently that it's really only Britain. If you take them out of Mexican heat and humidity and plonk them straight down into brisk and breezy Britain, they'll resent it greatly. Under these circumstances, growth becomes hard and often stops completely and it's quite difficult to get them growing again.

PRICKING OUT CONTAINER-GROWN SEEDLINGS.

1. The pot or tray of germinated seedlings will be very crowded. Once the first true leaves appear, the seedlings need more space.

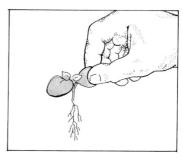

*2. Having made ready a tray of fresh compost, ease out the seedlings one by one, using a fine dibber or the point of a knife. Be sure not to damage the delicate root system, and hold the seedlings by the leaves, **not** the stem.*

3. Plant the seedlings in holes made in the compost using your finger or a thin stick. They need to be about 5 cm (2 in) from each other, and are best planted in rows so that you can easily remove the grown plants. Firm each seedling gently into the compost.

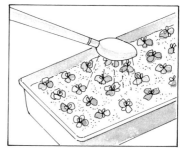

4. Water, using the fine rose on a watering can.

Multiple-sown onions jostle each other aside so that each forms a perfect plant.

So, before planting out into lower temperatures, wean them by putting them into a cold frame and gradually increasing the ventilation over a period of a couple of weeks at least.

Harvesting your own seed

A very satisfying way to produce new plants each season is to collect your own seed. You can propagate most plants like this including annuals, biennals, hardy perennials, trees, shrubs, bulbs, alpines and even vegetables.

Keep a careful eye on plants as they go out of flower because it's important to catch the seeds at the right time. When the seed-heads turn brown and the first one has fallen naturally, that's the time to collect the rest.

Choose a dry day and carefully cut each stem and put the heads into a paper bag. Bring them into a dry place and lay them out on sheets of paper to dry further. You'll often be able to shake the seed out but if you have to crush the seed-head to get at it, make sure you remove as much of the debris from the seed as possible since it's here that fungus diseases lurk.

Some seed can then be sown straightaway while some's best kept until spring and sown in gentle heat. As mentioned, the general rule of thumb is that half-hardy annuals and any tender perennials are best kept till spring but the rest can be sown straightaway. If in doubt divide the sample into two and do it both ways to be on the safe side. There's rarely a shortage of seed.

Of course, seed collection can be a gamble because there's nearly always a little variation in the resulting plants and often it can be very marked indeed. Some flowers that have been cross-pollinated by insects turn out to be useless but there's always the chance that others may be very good.

The only ones not really worth troubling with are the F1 hybrids which will almost certainly not be like the parent plant and will rarely be worthwhile (see page 153).

Overleaf, *harvesting your garden seeds for use next year is thrifty, as well as rewarding and satisfying.*

CHAPTER FIVE

A HEALTHY PLANT

Plants are designed for one reason only – to survive long enough to produce seed to contribute to the next generation. The stems, the leaves, the flowers and all that production of plant material are simply a means to that end. But that's just not good enough for us gardeners.

We want all our plants to thrive in the peak of condition. If we're growing leaf vegetables, for example, we want to prolong the vegetative phase of the plants' lives. We certainly don't want them to run to seed quickly. If it's flowers we're after, we're interested in perhaps prolonging flower production for as long as possible. It's only with fruiting plants that we're more or less in tune with nature's own plans.

Plant breeders have done much to provide us with the leafiest lettuce, the longest-flowering phlox and the most succulent strawberries but we still need to make our contribution to the husbandry of our plants. And for that we need to understand the different influences that go to make up a healthy plant.

GARDEN GEOGRAPHY

Modern gardens are an astonishing mixture of plants from all over the world and from many different habitats. And of course, being gardeners, most of us want to grow each and every plant that takes our fancy, whether it's naturally adapted to our conditions or not.

For example, two widely grown, native garden shrubs are quite exacting in their requirements in the wild. *Daphne mezereum* grows in woods on limy soils, while shrubby cinquefoil (*Potentilla fruticosa*) prefers damp, rocky slopes or it's sometimes found on shingle by rivers and lakes. Yet we expect both to survive in the open aridity of a typical suburban front garden.

To be successful with any plant, you should try to recreate as closely as possible its natural habitat. If you want to grow sundews and other bog plants, you must create a marshy patch with quite acid soil. If you prefer traditional meadow flowers like corncockle, corn marigold, knapweeds and poppies, you'll be most successful if you give them a dry area with few nutrients. Indeed, the way to establish a wildflower meadow is to remove the top-soil, sow on the much less fertile sub-soil, and then, when you mow the meadow, remove the 'hay' so that there's no build-up of soil nutrients which would encourage ranker vegetation that would smother the flowers.

In the average British garden you could travel the world without moving more than a few yards. Michaelmas daisies, *Rudbeckia* and goldenrod come from the meadows of North America, while lavender, rosemary, sage, thyme and other herbs hail from the coastal areas of southern Europe. South-west Asia gives us crocuses, mock orange, arabis and garden peas while buddleia, iceplant and clematis originated in China. Hydrangeas and privet are natives of Japan, and hollyhocks, chrysanthemums and asters grow wild in both China and Japan. Dahlias and so-called French marigolds actually come from Mexico, nasturtiums from Peru, and many other plants, such as runner beans, marrows, tomatoes and petunias from Central or South America. Rhubarb originated in Siberia, basil in India, lobelia and red-hot pokers in South Africa, and so it goes on.

We expect, and usually manage, to cultivate in our gardens hundreds of different plants from this vast range of habitats in many different countries. Even a sparse knowledge of their country of origin and the conditions under which they grow naturally, will help you make your plants feel at home and happy.

By and large, wherever it comes from originally, a healthy garden plant is sturdy and bushy, rather than slender and straggly, its leaves are a bright green, and its root system is well developed. Of course, you can think of exceptions, (no one wants their sunflowers to be bushy), but we still know what we expect in a healthy plant.

HOW PLANTS GROW

Growth in plants takes place principally at the tips of shoots and roots. New cells are continually formed by cell division, and as further division pushes them away from the growing point, they differentiate into cells with different functions, such as strengthening, water transport or sugar transport.

At the tip of the stem, the growing point gives rise to little clusters of cells which are the beginnings of leaves and these grow up to enclose and protect the growing point as the top or 'apical' bud. Eventually the main shoot grows out of the bud and leaves unfold down the length of the shoot. Further internal growth leads to the expansion and thickening of the stem.

Once the leaves of dicotyledons (with two seed leaves), which form the bulk of our garden plants, have unfurled, no further growth takes place in them. Cut off the end half of a leaf and it remains as half a leaf.

Grasses and the other monocotyledons, (one seed leaf), such as lilies, leeks and daffodils, are different, because their growing point is at the base of the leaf. When the end is cut, growth from the base makes good what has been removed. That's why, when you cut the lawn it continues to grow and will soon need cutting again.

BRANCHING GROWTH

When a shoot develops on a plant, the bud

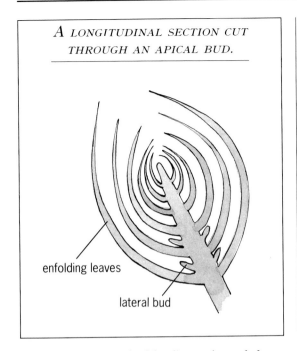

A LONGITUDINAL SECTION CUT THROUGH AN APICAL BUD.

enfolding leaves

lateral bud

at the end (the apical bud) consists of the growing tip of the shoot and the inwardly curved leaves that protect it. As the shoot grows and the leaves unfurl, you can usually see a tiny bud in the joint where each leaf joins the stem. In normal circumstances, few if any of these buds develop. If, however, the top bud is damaged or removed, these lateral buds develop into side branches. That's because the top bud sends a growth suppressing substance down to the other buds to stop them growing out. This is known as 'apical dominance' and it's there to enable plants to grow up quickly to reach the light. We gardeners make use of this information, whether or not we realise it, when we prune trees and shrubs or 'stop' runner beans or chrysanthemums (see pages 154–7). By removing the top bud we take away the growth retarding hormone so side branches develop, and we get bushy growth.

In a more pronounced way, the same thing happens when you clip a hedge. With the suppressant effects of apical dominance removed, not just in leading shoots, but on all the side branches as well, the plant thickens out and hundreds of side shoots develop.

The same growth retarding hormone has a rather different effect on stems. It will stimulate the growth of lateral roots from the stem rather than from the main root, and it won't surprise you to learn that the substance is used in what we know as hormone rooting powder.

You may wonder why, if apical dominance has such a strong effect, plants ever spontaneously develop side shoots. Well, the answer seems to be that plants also produce other hormones which have a powerful effect on growth. These hormones are known by the improbable name of 'gibberellins', after a fungus called *Gibberella* which produces substances that have the same effect.

Plant growth is an intricate and complex process and depends on the health of every part of the plant and of all the cells involved. To have a healthy, productive plant, we have to ensure that it gets everything it needs and is grown in optimum conditions, free of damaging influences.

WATER

The first and perhaps the most obvious need of plants is water. Without it they wilt, leaves and young shoots die off, and ultimately the whole plant collapses. You can see the effect best in a soft plant like an annual or a herbaceous plant but it's just as true for those with woody, supporting tissue, like trees. A dead tree doesn't necessarily collapse because the tough, woody tissue holds up the trunk and supports the branches. But sooner or later, branches break and fall, the dead roots lose their grip on the soil, and the trunk topples.

We gardeners have to ensure that the soil around the roots remains moist but in dry

summer conditions that's not easy to judge. Roots go down a long way into the soil, and dryness of the soil surface is no guide to what's happening underneath. Soil enriched by organic matter will hold water better and stay moist for much longer than inorganic soil with none.

Ideally, water in the evening so that during the night the water can soak down into the soil before the sun's heat starts

Shrubby cinquefoil Potentilla fruticosa *grows wild in Britain on damp, rocky slopes or on shingle by rivers and lakes.*

Opposite, *a wildflower meadow growing on dry soil poor in nutrients includes ox-eye daisies (white), corn marigolds (yellow), knapweeds (blue), poppies (red) and corncockles (pink).*

Below, *sweetly-scented* Daphne mezereum *grows wild in Britain in woods on limy soil. Like* Potentilla fruticosa, *it is rare.*

evaporating it. And make sure you water the soil rather than the foliage because though the leaves take up some water it's negligible compared with what goes through the roots. What's more, dowsing a warm plant with cold water on a hot day will be a damaging shock.

Don't be in too much of a hurry to start watering in a dry spell. Plant roots naturally go down to seek water but an abundance of water at the soil surface encourages shallow rooting and so the plant won't need to go deeper. Start watering too early in the summer and you only create a situation in which you have to go on watering – perhaps daily! And when you do start, make sure you soak the soil well or, again, the roots stay at the top where they're even more prone to drying out.

Mulching with compost, bark chippings, straw or even black polythene helps retain water by cutting evaporation from the surface, a process that, once started, tends to draw water from deeper and deeper in the soil.

Plants need plenty of moisture because the green parts consist of 90 per cent water, which has to be maintained. Water is also one of the raw materials of photosynthesis, the process by which plants make sugars (see page 95) and ultimately all the other complex chemical compounds of which they consist. So, without water, there would be no plant. It's as simple as that.

If a plant is to stay erect and all its green tissues are to stay firm, the individual cells must be turgid like little balloons full of fluid. If water is withdrawn from the cells as happens when it's hot and dry and there's much evaporation through the pores on the undersides of the leaves, or when the plant has no water the cells collapse and the plant wilts.

If the cells do collapse the pores automatically close off so that there's no more water loss. So, to some extent, wilting is protective although it should be corrected as soon as possible.

The pores are an essential part of the structure of leaves because they take in and breathe out the carbon dioxide and oxygen that are used for photosynthesis and for respiration. In daylight, a plant takes in carbon dioxide more rapidly than it uses oxygen while at night the reverse is true.

A very magnified view of the underside of a leaf showing pores through which carbon dioxide, oxygen and water vapour pass.

Water is also constantly lost through the pores by evaporation and the losses are made good by taking more up through the roots. So there's a constant stream of water through the plant. And, if you've ever wondered why you need to keep carting that watering can backwards and forwards in the summer, you should know that an oak tree takes up about 680 litres (150 gallons) of water a day while a sunflower absorbs 200 litres (44 gallons) during its six-month life.

Plants take water from the soil mainly through microscopically fine structures called root hairs that grow out about 4 millimetres (1/6 inch) from just behind the growing tip of each root. These very fine rootlets are essential since only they take up water. So when you're planting anything with bare roots make sure that they're never allowed to dry out in the wind or sun.

Water passes through the tissues of the root into centrally placed water vessels, which are long, hollow cells placed end to end up the root and stem. Water continually moves up these cells, partly because of the pull caused by evaporation from leaves, and partly because by absorbing the water the roots actually push it up. It's due to this root pressure that the stump of a lopped tree 'bleeds' water, sometimes for days.

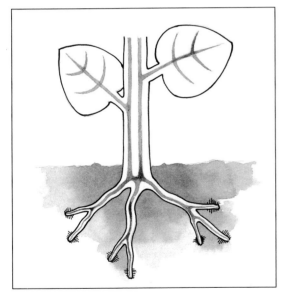

The water-conducting system is continuous from the roots up to the top of stems and leaves.

This continual upwards flow of water is very important to the plant, not least because nutrients are carried in the water. Furthermore, the evaporation from leaf surfaces has a cooling effect that is particularly important in hot, dry conditions. You can't, of course, see evaporation from leaves but its magnitude is indicated by the way excess water is exuded and drips from the leaves of some plants on warm, humid days, or at night when evaporation is impossible.

LIGHT AND THE PLANT

Every gardener knows that plants need light. A plant grown in darkness is spindly, yellow and looks pretty unhealthy. Only in light does it develop normally bushy growth and a good green colour.

First of all, light is used to help make sugars, which plants need just as much as we do. They do it by a process known as photosynthesis, which takes place in the green parts of plants, mainly the leaves. Making a complex substance like sugar from simple things like water and carbon dioxide takes a lot of energy, which plants get from the light that shines on their leaves. Part of the process takes place in light, and a second stage happens in the dark. In the light stage, water is split into its component parts, hydrogen and oxygen, while light energy is changed into chemical energy. The oxygen formed is given off by the plant, and that's why submerged water plants give off bubbles of gas in sunlight.

The hydrogen and chemical energy are then used in the dark stage to convert carbon dioxide to sugar. The amount of energy absorbed from the sun and used is quite mind-boggling when you realise that to form a pound of sugar a plant uses the same amount of energy needed to boil four gallons of water.

Photosynthesis takes place in the green parts of the plant, mainly the leaves, and the green colour comes from a substance called chlorophyll. This is also only made

Colourful nasturtiums originated in Peru but are now widely grown in gardens.

Stately hollyhocks come from China and Japan. Pollinated by bumble-bees, they seed freely in gardens.

Like many of the aromatic plants we grow, lavender grows wild in the Mediterranean region.

in light, which is why plants raised in the dark are pale yellow. Interestingly, chlorophyll absorbs and uses mainly light in the red and blue parts of the spectrum, reflecting green light which, of course, is why plants look green. Variegated plants don't have chlorophyll in the white areas of their leaves, which means that they're less able to make sugars and that's why they grow less vigorously than all-green plants.

Light is also necessary for various other functions. Plants respond to light by releasing materials that cause the stems, leaves and roots to grow and expand and the flowers to develop. But it's worth noting that different plants have different light requirements, and you can't necessarily improve the condition of all plants by giving them more. Some grow better in shade while others are best in full sunshine.

In woodland, most low-growing plants are adapted to function at low light levels because for most of the year they're shaded by the trees above. The leaves of many of them limit the amount of carbon dioxide that can enter the pores and diffuse into

Magnified view of the fine root hairs which take up water into plants.

the working cells. This limits the rate of photosynthesis, and no amount of extra light would benefit them. Indeed, it may be positively harmful since the plant would get hotter and lose more water by evaporation. A well-known example is greenback in tomatoes grown too close to the greenhouse glass.

As you'd expect, many shade-lovers are woodland species – plants such as primroses, hellebores, trilliums, lily-of the-valley and

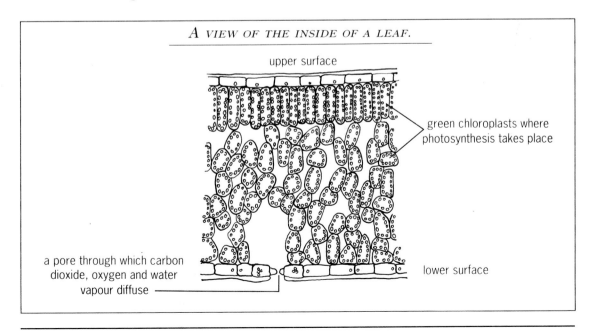

A VIEW OF THE INSIDE OF A LEAF.

upper surface

green chloroplasts where photosynthesis takes place

a pore through which carbon dioxide, oxygen and water vapour diffuse

lower surface

Red-hot pokers Kniphofia *grow wild in South Africa. Once established, they grow well in a sunny spot and can withstand dry conditions. In cold winters, they need some protection.*

Lilies-of-the-valley are plants of English woodland which grow early in the year.

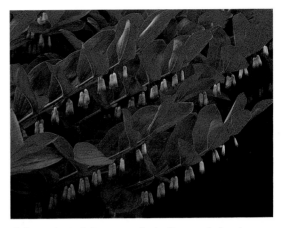

Solomon's seal flowers early in the year before trees cast their full shadow.

Hellebores are also woodland plants which can be used in the garden for underplanting beneath trees. They prefer partial shade because there is less water loss from their leaves.

Solomon's seal. Under natural conditions, however, they make most of their growth early in the year, before the trees above them cast their full shadow. So, in the garden they'll do better in the shade of trees than they would if they were shaded permanently by the house. A number of herbaceous garden plants grow best in partial shade because of the lower water loss from their leaves. Giant bellflower (*Campanula latifolia*), leopard's bane (*Doronicum*), black false hellebore (*Veratrum nigrum*) and plume poppies (*Macleaya*) do better at the back of a border where the leaves are shaded. Shrubs like camellias, rhododendrons and mahonias grow in the wild at the edge of woodland so they prefer partial, dappled shade.

We all know that shoots and stems grow towards light, while roots either grow away from it or don't respond at all.

The shoots of plants shaded on one side, or pot plants on a windowsill in a dark room, bend towards the light, and this can be corrected by turning the pot daily. What happens is that a growth hormone, or auxin, produced in the shoot tip accumulates on the shaded side, where it causes more growth, hence the bend towards the light.

Growth in leaf stalks is also affected by light, so that all the leaves of a plant face the light and, as far as possible, don't shade each other.

The number of hours of daylight they receive also influences plants, particularly their flowering. Commercial growers make use of this knowledge by adjusting the length of day plants are subjected to by using black polythene screens and special lights so that, for instance, poinsettias and chrysanthemums are induced to flower at Christmas.

Some plants are called long-day plants because they only flower when the days are long and nights short. Not surprisingly, these are mostly plants that flower in the summer or grow wild in temperate regions, and include spinach, radish, lettuce, petunias, *Rudbeckia*, *Phacelia*, evening primrose, irises, sweet williams, love-in-a-mist and catchfly.

Others, mainly those that grow wild nearer the equator or flower in winter or spring, require short days and long nights. These include chrysanthemums, poinsettias, dahlias, *Cosmos* and tobacco. The so-called 'day-neutral' plants like tomato, cotton and many of our weeds are indifferent to day length and flower at all seasons.

TEMPERATURE

Temperature has a great effect on plant growth, and the ideal growing and flowering temperature depends on what part of the world the plant comes from. As you would expect, most tropical plants germinate and subsequently flower at much higher temperatures than temperate ones.

Generally, a rise in temperature means an increase in growth. This is because chemical processes are involved, and an increase in temperature speeds up the rate of chemical reactions. Obviously though, there are limits and few plants will grow at temperatures below 5°C (41°F) or above 25°C (77°F). All grow best between 10° and 25°C (50°–77°F).

Freezing temperatures damage the foliage of most plants because ice crystals rupture the cells, which can then no longer function. Freezing removes free water and thus also has a drying and damaging effect. Because it effectively dries out, new 'sappy' growth is more prone to frost damage than mature shoots which contain less water. This is also the main reason why really good drainage will help plants survive a cold winter because there is less water around.

Plants with a high sugar content will also survive better in lower temperatures. If plants grown in warmer conditions are gradually and progressively subjected to cooler temperatures, their sugar content increases, and this is one of the reasons why 'hardening off' of seedlings is so essential when they're taken from the warm greenhouse to the cooler garden.

Never forget too, that sudden temperature shocks are bad for most plants. That's why you should never dowse foliage with cold water from the hose on a hot day, and why a late frost may kill a plant that has withstood a severe winter.

Sometimes the damaging effects of a late frost or the death of a plant in one part of the garden and not one of the same species growing elsewhere, is due to 'cold air drainage'. Cold air tends to sink, whereas warmer air rises, so there's a flow of cold air to the lowest part of the garden. This produces so-called 'frost pockets'. Often, planting on a raised bed or a slight mound is all that's necessary to protect a tender plant.

A cloche or other covering, or a light mulch of straw or something similar will also protect tender growth from frost, and the old stems of herbaceous plants left standing through the winter will deflect cold air from the emerging shoots. These will also be protected by fallen leaves so don't be in too much of a hurry to 'tidy up' the garden in the autumn.

Gardeners sometimes 'force' plants to develop earlier than normal by raising their temperature as is done in greenhouses or on old-fashioned hotbeds. By and large this will only work if the plant is ready to grow and not in a dormant phase. In other words, it's almost impossible to alter the normal course of development although you can speed it up.

High temperatures can damage many plants. In extreme cases, death is caused by the coagulation of proteins in the cells – the plant literally cooks. The more usual problem from hot weather is that the plant loses too much water, so it wilts (see page 94).

It's also worth noting that if flowers are cut on a hot day when there's a rapid upward passage of water through the plant, air instead of water is sucked into the cut stalks and, when the stems are put in water in a vase, air bubbles clog them so that the flowers visibly wilt. This can usually be avoided by slitting or cutting the flower stalks just before putting in water.

NUTRIENTS

As well as carbon dioxide, oxygen, water, light and a certain degree of warmth, plants need food. It's absorbed through their roots as a solution of salts, the most important nutrients being nitrogen, phosphorus and potassium. Plants also need calcium, magnesium, sulphur and the so-called 'trace elements' – manganese, boron, zinc, copper, iron, and molybdenum – which are needed in only minute amounts.

Nitrogen is a necessary constituent of all proteins and is the element needed for good leaf and stem growth. Phosphorus is essential to provide energy in all living cells and is mainly responsible for healthy root growth. Potassium is necessary for good flowering and fruit formation.

Calcium is a vital constituent of plant cell walls – the plant's 'skeleton' if you like – which is why watercress which grows in chalk streams is so brittle and crunchy. Other uses of essential elements in plants and symptoms of deficiencies are in the table on page 105.

Leopard's bane Doronicum, *a native to Britain, grows wild in woods, so in the garden prefers the back of a border where there is partial shade.*

Love-in-a-mist Nigella damascena, *from the Mediterranean, is a long-day plant, which only flowers when days are long and nights short. Dead-heading prolongs flowering.*

Essential elements can sometimes interact as, for example, when excess potassium 'locks up' calcium or magnesium in the soil, making it unavailable to plants and causing deficiency. Uptake of elements may also be influenced by the pH (acidity) of the soil. For instance, lime-hating plants cannot get iron and other trace elements from alkaline soils.

Because all these mineral elements are absorbed through the plant's roots, if you want to treat the deficiency you need to treat the soil. If you see signs of nitrogen deficiency, use a high-nitrogen fertiliser like dried blood; treat a phosphorus deficiency with a dressing of bonemeal; and correct a potassium deficiency with rock potash. In practice, it's generally only these major elements you need to worry about, provided you incorporate lots of manure or compost to build up a balanced nutrient level in the soil. All trace element deficiencies can be treated with liquid seaweed, followed by a dressing of seaweed meal. It is, however, worth pointing out that if a boron deficiency becomes apparent, it's too late to save the crop, although treatment will ensure that the next one doesn't suffer similarly.

PLANT DISEASES

In a well-run garden, where the plants grow strongly and healthily with adequate space, food and water, there should be few problems with plant disease caused by fungi, bacteria or viruses.

Every effort should be made to create a healthy garden by good cultivation methods to produce strong, hardy plants, because the last thing you want to do is to practise chemical warfare. All insecticides and fungicides are indiscriminate in what they kill and will harm your friends and allies as well as your enemies.

Still, you must bear in mind that the spores of fungus diseases are floating around in the air most of the time. Bacteria are also everywhere and viruses are carried by insects, especially greenfly. You can't see disease spores and you can't stop them but you can grow plants that are hard and healthy and will shrug them off. Just as a weak, underfed child will be prey to every disease under the sun, so puny, badly brought up plants will suffer too.

The first step is to grow strong plants that have had enough to eat and drink but have never been coddled with excessive doses of junk food in the form of chemical fertilisers.

An eagle eye helps too. As soon as you see the first signs of alien marks on leaves, pick the affected leaves off and get rid of them. Put them in a polythene bag and throw them in the dustbin.

Bear in mind too, that diseases often attack native plants first so keep your garden as weed-free as you can and remove dead and dying plant material straightaway.

Finally, we can use our own natural defence mechanism here too – our intelligence. One of the most important priorities of modern plant breeding is freedom from disease. Scientists have, over the years, produced many plant varieties that show varying degrees of resistance. There are lettuces that don't get mildew, parsnips that fight off canker, strawberries, tomatoes and cucumbers that are resistant to virus diseases, roses that are hardly, if at all, prone to blackspot and many, many more. Now we are able to transfer genes from one species to another by genetic engineering, we're likely to see much more breeding for health. (We both have our reservations about the wisdom of tinkering with nature in this particular way but we shall have to see.)

So, if you're buying plants that are notoriously affected by disease, choose resistant varieties wherever possible. Avoid blackspotty roses like Dearest and shun mildew apples like Cox but buy mildewless lettuce like Avondefiance and brown-rot-resistant tomatoes like Piranto.

Use of mineral elements by plants and symptoms of deficiency

NITROGEN Essential constituent of proteins, so necessary for growth; especially important for leafy growth; also present in other important cell chemicals.
Deficiency causes thin, upright, spindly growth with few laterals and small, pale green leaves; fruit trees lose leaves and have few blossoms; small, hard apples.

PHOSPHORUS Vital for energy exchange, including photosynthesis and respiration; present in many proteins, fats and carbohydrates, and in chromosomes; especially important in root growth, ripening of fruits, maturation and germination of seeds.
Deficiency causes poor, spindly growth and discoloured leaves (dull bluish-green, purple or bronzed); soft, acid apples.

POTASSIUM Essential for good flowers and fruit formation; probably involved with photosynthesis and control of water loss; important in leaves and growing points; helps to ripen and harden plant tissues.
Deficiency causes 'scorching' of leaf edges, poor, thin growth often with death of whole fruit tree branches, poor flowers, tasteless, woody fruit.

CALCIUM Essential constituent of plant cell walls; necessary for correct functioning of growth points and other young tissues.
Deficiency (often a case of plant's inability to distribute it through system) causes blossom-end rot in tomatoes, tip-burn in lettuce, black heart in celery, browning in centre of Brussels sprouts.

MAGNESIUM Contained in chlorophyll and therefore essential for photosynthesis.
Deficiency causes chlorosis (yellowing between leaf veins).

SULPHUR Found in certain proteins.
Deficiency causes stunting and yellowing.

MANGANESE Concerned with chlorophyll formation.
Deficiency causes stunting of young leaves and chlorosis.

BORON Concerned with making calcium available to plant tissues; especially important in growing tissue.
Deficiency causes internal 'corkiness' in apples and root crops, brown-heart in celery and brassicas.

ZINC Essential for correct functioning of some enzymes.
Deficiency causes yellow mottling on young leaves.

COPPER Essential for correct functioning of some enzymes.
Deficiency causes yellow mottling on young leaves.

IRON Required for the synthesis of chlorophyll; present in compounds involved with energy release.
Deficiency causes yellowing between veins.

MOLYBDENUM Involved in utilisation of nitrogen.
Deficiency causes poor growth of shoots and roots.

Roses are subject to black-spot disease but blooms like these are a sure sign of a healthy plant.

Poinsettias are short-day plants which special light regimes induce to flower at Christmas.

Opposite, *healthy hydrangeas like these are pink on limy soils but blue when grown on acid soils.*

CHAPTER SIX

POLLINATION –
CONTINUING THE LINE

We gardeners prize all parts of plants for one reason or another. It may be decorative or tasty foliage, beautiful flowers or even edible roots, but for the plant itself all these are only a means to an end. All it's interested in is the production of seed to get it into the next generation and so to ensure the survival of the species.

To achieve that end plants need to produce seed and, like most living things, that requires the union of male and female. But because they're rooted to the spot and can't move around to find a mate they have to employ a go-between to transfer the male pollen to the female ovaries. This could simply be gravity or wind since some plants carry both male and female flowers and most flowers are both male and female, or they could attract insects or other animals to carry pollen between flowers on different plants.

Of course, setting seed is often the last thing the gardener wants. Certainly no one's pleased to see their lettuces or cabbages run to seed and so become useless in the kitchen.

And sometimes it's quite immaterial to the gardener whether the flowers are pollinated or not since it's often the flowers themselves that are the gardeners' end-product.

But on many occasions good pollination and a heavy set of fruit and seed is very much in our interest. There would, of course, be no apples or pears, tomatoes or strawberries without pollination. Neither would there be attractive end-of-season berries or the striking seed-heads of teazel, honesty and poppies, so much in demand by flower arrangers. But, perhaps more important, there would be no seed of favourite flowers and vegetables to save and none of those self-set seedlings that prove so interesting to gardeners.

So, it's very much in our interests to provide the best conditions possible for pollination.

HOW IT WORKS

Pollen is transferred from the male parts (the stamens) to the female part (the stigma) of the same flower or a different one of the same species. Both parts can be found in the central area of the flower, generally surrounded by the petals, (though some flowers like grass have no petals).

Usually stamens consist of a flexible stalk and an attached, lobe-shaped structure on top that produces the grains of pollen. There may be as few as two, as in sage flowers (see page 120), or a great cluster of them, as in poppies.

The stigma is the sticky tip of the structure that extends out from an ovary, and it's the ovary that contains the little ovules which are destined to become seeds. Some flowers, such as those of peas and beans, have one ovary and stigma whereas others, such as buttercups, have several.

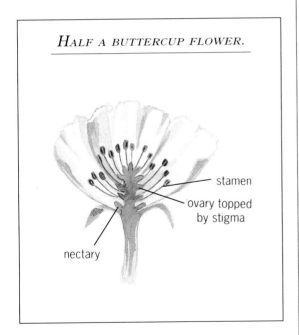

HALF A BUTTERCUP FLOWER.

stamen

ovary topped by stigma

nectary

Before the ovules can be fertilised to become seeds, the flowers have to be pollinated. Pollen grains contain what can be thought of as male sex cells, the equivalent of sperm in animals, whereas the ovules in a flower's ovary contain the female sex cells, which are effectively eggs.

When a pollen grain alights on a receptive stigma it starts to grow, developing a pollen tube which works its way down into the ovary and enters an ovule. Once there, the tip of the pollen tube ruptures, releasing two male sex cells, one of which then fuses with the female sex cell giving rise to a fertilised seed. The other fuses with other material in the ovule to produce eventually the food stores of the seed.

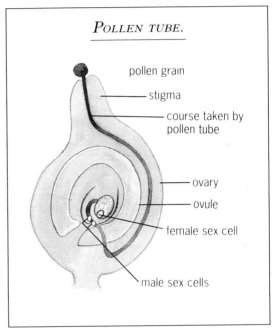

POLLEN TUBE.

pollen grain

stigma

course taken by pollen tube

ovary

ovule

female sex cell

male sex cells

A pollen tube, down which the male sex cells travel, grows from a pollen grain down the stigma and into an ovule within the ovary.

As in animals, the sex cells contain only half the genes of the plant so it is only after fertilisation that the full genetic complement is restored. Usually, any harmful genetic characteristics in one plant are cancelled out by those in the other, and it's obviously desirable that this should be so. But when a plant is self-pollinated and so fertilises its own seeds, there's a risk that there will be a double dose of any bad genes.

*The striking seed-heads of honesty (**left**) are much in demand by flower-arrangers. The flowers of sweet vernal grass (**above**) and fox-tail grass (**below**) are not showy but liberate vast amounts of pollen from their prominent stamens.*

Cross-pollination with another plant is highly desirable so over time plants have evolved a variety of mechanisms to prevent self-pollination, or at least to make it less likely.

Sometimes the male and female parts of a flower mature at different times. Often, the stigma grows above the stamens and out of the way of falling pollen. Some plants, such as cucumbers, have separate male and female flowers, and in others, such as most hollies, the male and female flowers are borne on separate plants. In many species self-pollination simply doesn't lead to self-fertilisation, often because the pollen tube doesn't develop properly.

However, self-fertilisation is better than leaving no offspring at all so many plant species have evolved a balance between self- and cross-pollination.

WIND POLLINATION

Wind-pollinated flowers are, to the gardener's eye, rather dull. They have no perfume and the petals are either very reduced or absent altogether, whereas the stamens and stigma are large and well exposed. Although close inspection reveals an intricate beauty, they're certainly not showy. Grasses, conifers, plantains, many of our commonest trees such as oak and ash, and a variety of other plants like sweetcorn are all wind-pollinated.

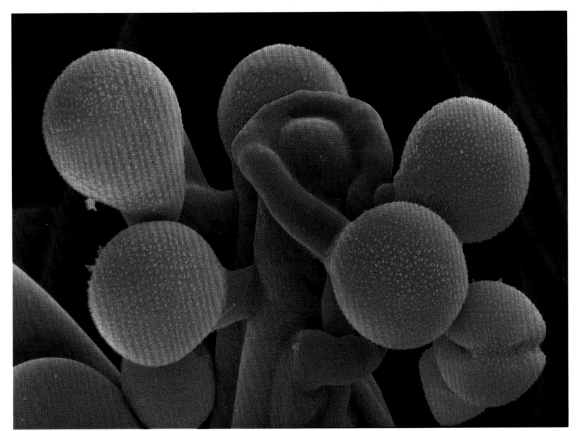

False-colour electron micrograph of pollen grains germinating on a stigma. Several pollen tubes are visible, one encircling the top of the stigma before growing down towards the base of the flower.

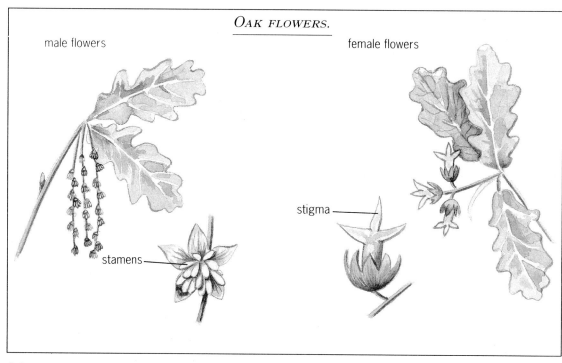

*Oak trees carry two sorts of flowers: male (**above left**) and female (**above right**).*

The casual blowing by the wind of pollen from one flower to another is a pretty haphazard process, and it depends for success on the production of enormous quantities of pollen. Hay-fever sufferers will be only too painfully aware of this. Each of the tiny florets that makes up a flowering spike of rye produces over 50,000 pollen grains, and a single birch catkin (and there are thousands on a tree) produces an incredible five and a half million.

Such a deluge of pollen is released by every puff of breeze that stigmas close to their own ripe stamens would be absolutely smothered, to the exclusion of pollen from other plants. So there have to be safeguards. One of these is for the stigma and stamens to mature at different times.

The other main safeguard is for the stamens and stigma to be placed apart, either because male and female flowers are separate, as in birches, or because male and female flowers are on separate trees, as in willows.

On many trees which are wind pollinated, the flowers appear early in spring, before the leaves, so that pollen has free access to the flowers.

INSECTS AND FLOWERS

Pollen is nutritious as a food so beetles, hoverflies, bees and other insects visit flowers to eat pollen or, in the case of bees, to collect it for their larvae to eat. Inevitably, such flower visitors not only eat pollen but also help transfer it from flower to flower so plants have capitalised on this convenient habit by evolving colourful, fragrant, nectar-producing flowers to attract insects.

Neither nectar, showy petals, nor sweet

scents serve any function in a plant's life except in pollination. Nectar is simply bait for insects or, in some tropical flowers, for birds, bats or other small mammals. Conspicuous petals and perfumes are labels that advertise the whereabouts of nectar and attract insects to it.

The pollen of insect-pollinated flowers is sticky so insect visitors inadvertently pick it up on their heads, bodies, legs, wings and mouthparts. When they then visit another flower they transfer it. Of course, there will be times when they're carrying the wrong pollen but generally nectar-feeding insects tend to be consistent, in the short term, to one species of flower. Obviously, if the feeding's good at one flower, it makes sense for visiting insects to seek out another one of the same sort.

Some flowers, like buddleia, are visited by a wide range of different types of insects. Others, like sage, are adapted to particular sorts of pollinators. In all, however, the insect is visiting the flowers for food, whether it be nectar or pollen, and the transfer of pollen is inadvertent as far as the insect is concerned. And that's exactly what the flowers are designed for so it's they that have the last laugh.

BEES AND POLLEN

Bees are terrific pollinators and the average garden may well have several different sorts including our native bumble-bees, and a whole range of solitary bees, as well as visiting honey-bees.

Bumble-bees, like honey-bees, are social insects. Nests are founded in spring by an overwintered queen, which raises a brood of infertile female workers that then take over all the workload of the nest except egg-laying, which remains the duty of the queen.

During the summer, more workers are produced and then, as autumn approaches, a brood of virgin queens and males. They leave the nest and mating takes place, the nest disintegrates, workers, males and the old queen die, and only newly fertilised queens survive the winter. All through the season, nectar and pollen are constantly brought back to the nest to feed the developing brood.

Solitary bees, on the other hand, have no social life. The female lawn-bee, for example, makes an isolated nesting cell in a burrow in a bare patch in the lawn. She stocks it with pollen moistened with nectar, on which she lays an egg. The egg hatches into a larva that eats the pollen and nectar, and then pupates in its cell, not emerging until the following year. There's no contact between a female and her offspring – they're truly solitary.

Bumble-bees, like honey-bees, have special structures on their hindmost legs for transporting pollen back to the nest. One of the lower sections of the leg is smooth, concave and surrounded by strong, incurving hairs forming a pollen basket.

HIND LEG OF A BUMBLE-BEE SHOWING POLLEN BASKET.

pollen basket

A colourful perennial garden. Conspicuous petals and perfumes are labels that advertise the whereabouts of nectar.

Buddleia is visited by a wide range of different insects attracted by its fruity scent.

Sweet pea flowers are usually self-pollinated.

Male birch catkins each release $5\frac{1}{2}$ million pollen grains.

The bees use their other legs to comb sticky pollen from the hairs that cover their bodies, and use their legs and mouthparts to pack the pollen into their baskets. When full, the bulging pollen baskets make it look as though the bee's wearing a pair of yellow or orange pantaloons.

Solitary bees too are covered with hairs and usually have pollen baskets, although they're just clusters of hairs and not so specialised.

The thing all the bees have in common is their covering of feathery, branched hairs, which pick up much pollen whenever the bee visits a flower. Not all the pollen is transferred to the pollen baskets, and bees out foraging are always well-coated with pollen which they inevitably transfer from flower to flower.

The villains of the piece in this otherwise benign world are the cuckoo-bees, which occupy the nests and steal the food stores of other bees. They're much less hairy and have no pollen baskets since they never collect and transport pollen.

OTHER INSECT POLLINATORS

Hoverflies are such regular flower visitors that in the USA they're called 'flower flies'. They eat both nectar and pollen, some species taking more of one, some more of the other. Most hoverflies have smooth, rather shiny surfaces to their bodies but even some of these smooth-bodied species are known to transfer pollen from one plant to another as they're feeding.

Others, such as the large drone fly, which looks superficially like a honey-bee, are quite hairy and it seems certain that they pick up and transfer pollen from flower to flower. As hoverflies, like bees, show consistency in the sort of flower they visit they're undoubtedly good pollinators.

The bodies of many moths are covered with hair-like scales and they inevitably pick up pollen on their bodies, heads, legs and scaly wings as they visit flowers to suck up nectar with their long tongues. It's worth going out into the garden with a torch on a warm, still night during the late summer to see just how many hundreds of moths are visiting the flowers. One common moth, the Silver-Y, which has a Y-shaped silver mark on each fore-wing, can often be seen feeding by day, flitting from flower to flower.

Any of the insects that visit flowers, such as butterflies and even shiny, hard-bodied beetles, must from time to time be involved in pollen transfer but the pollinators *par excellence* are undoubtedly the bees.

BUMBLE-BEES AND FOXGLOVES

For most of the summer bumble-bees are the most conspicuous garden animals, and they're the main pollinators of many garden flowers. The largest bumble-bees can get right inside the flowers of foxgloves, for example, so that only intermittent, high-pitched buzzing betrays their presence. The bell-shaped flowers have a conspicuous landing platform, liberally speckled with white-ringed, dark purple markings that guide a bee to the nectaries at the base of the petal tube.

White foxgloves appear to have only a few brownish speckles but they probably have nectar-guides that reflect ultra-violet light. Bees see only the shorter wavelengths so they can see ultra-violet but not red. When photographed with special ultra-violet sensitive film, many flowers prove to have nectar guides that would be conspicuous to bees but not to us.

The structure of foxglove flowers favours cross-pollination. The stigma and stamens of newly opened flowers fit snugly against the upper part of the bell, and the lobes at the ends of the stamens are pressed together, preventing release of the fine pollen. As a bumble-bee delves into a flower for nectar and presses against the stamen bases, the lobes separate, showering the visitor with pollen.

In older flowers, the stamens are well-separated and curve round the sides of the bell, while the stigma bends downwards so that it brushes the back of entering bees, picking up any pollen they carry.

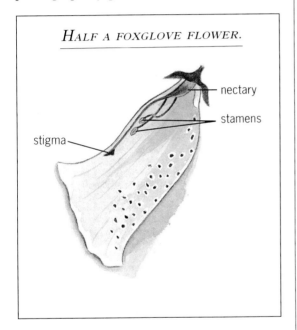

Half a foxglove flower.

nectary

stamens

stigma

Insects' tongues

It's fascinating that both insects and flowers have evolved to become mutually dependent. This has resulted in certain 'specialities' with some insects preferring certain types of flower and some flowers adapting their structure to suit certain insects.

Different species of bumble-bees have tongues of differing lengths. Those with the longest ones, particularly white-tailed bumble-bees, have no trouble reaching down into deep, rather narrow flowers like comfrey and columbines. It's mainly the blue and purple flowers that tend to have their nectar hidden deep in the flower, and these are the speciality of the long-tongued bees.

Short-tongued species, like many of the solitary bees, the beetles, flies and some moths, visit flowers whose nectar is easier to get at, like buttercups. They seem to favour white or yellow flowers.

The nectar in rowan flowers is completely exposed and accessible to all. Although the flowers are small, they're massed into conspicuous, flat bunches over which visiting insects can range freely.

The flowers of daisies and similar plants are really a mass of tubular florets packed together. Their florets are shallow and their nectar can be reached by short-tongued insects but other plants such as cornflowers and thistles have deep florets so consequently are visited by long-tongued bees and butterflies.

Flowers that attract butterflies and moths, like valerian, *Nicotiana* and various sorts of *Phlox* and *Dianthus*, are a bit more restricted in their clientele than bee flowers because their petal tubes are too narrow and deep for anything other than a long, thin tongue.

Most insects can feed from a great range of flowers but the deeper the nectar is in a flower the more restricted is the range of insects that can feed from it, and therefore pollinate it.

Flowers that attract moths are most attractive in the evening when the moths are first on the wing looking for food. *Nicotiana* and honeysuckle seem to glow in the half-light and their scents seem particularly strong. At this time too, the

Opposite above, *silver-Y moths are abundant migrants which can often be seen by day flitting from flower to flower or feeding on fruit juices. Covered with powdery scales, they function as excellent pollinators.*

Opposite below, *drone flies* Eristalis tenax, *like other hoverflies, feed at flowers. Being hairy, they become smothered with pollen, which they transfer to other flowers.*

Left, *the petal tubes of* Phlox paniculata *are too narrow and deep for anything other than a long, thin tongue. They attract and are pollinated by butterflies and moths.*

Below, *hummingbird hawkmoths feed by day as well as at night. Their wings transfer pollen by brushing against stamens and stigma as they hover in front of many flowers.*

production of nectar also reaches a peak. Take an evening stroll in the garden and you may be lucky enough to see hawk moths pollinating the elegant flowers of Turk's-cap and madonna lilies. Their wings transfer pollen by brushing against the projecting stamens and stigma as they hover in front of the flowers sucking up nectar with their long tongues.

Flowers depend on bees and other insects for pollination, while butterflies, moths, bees, hoverflies and a host of other insects depend on flowers for food in the form of nectar and pollen. So they're mutually dependent; neither could exist without the other. It's not surprising then that the association between particular sorts of insects and a particular flower has become very close, with flowers adapted in shape and structure to their insect visitors. The association between sage flowers and bumble-bees is a perfect example.

SAGE AND BUMBLE-BEES

Individual purplish-blue sage flowers could not be better designed for pollination by bumble-bees. The petal that forms the broad lower lip serves as a landing platform. The purple and white streaks in the throat guide visitors to the nectaries at the base of the flower tube.

The stamens (two of them) are each shaped a bit like an old-fashioned telephone receiver, attached by a hinge at the middle. The pollen-bearing lobes at one end lie in the throat of the flower, while those at the other end are concealed beneath the upper, hood-shaped petal. As a bee delves into the flower it pushes against the lower ends of the stamens so that the upper ends swing down in a see-saw action and strike it on the back, covering it with pollen. In freshly-opened flowers, the stigma is above the

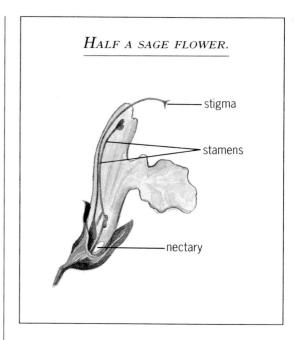

HALF A SAGE FLOWER.

stigma

stamens

nectary

stamens within the hood but in older flowers it curves downwards and visiting bees brush against it, transferring any pollen on their backs.

Bumble-bees are the only insects with tongues long enough to reach the nectar, and bulky enough to fill the flower entrance so that they operate the stamen mechanism and brush against the stigma.

The tall spikes of purplish-blue sage flowers that are so conspicuous in June hum then with the comings and goings of bumble-bees.

Tightly-packed pollen baskets are clearly visible on many of the visitors but the success of their activities as pollinators is evident later in the year, when the old flowering spikes rattle with round black seeds.

HONEYSUCKLE AND MOTHS

Honeysuckle flowers are admirably adapted for pollination by night-flying moths and they're visited by hawk moths and by the

Silver-Y. Each 'flower' is really a cluster of long-tubed, pale, sweet-scented flowers, each with long, projecting stamens and stigma. On the first evening of opening, the flowers are clear, creamy-white in colour and they give out a powerful perfume until after nightfall.

The pollen-bearing lobes of the projecting stamens are directly in front of the petal tube so that they're in the path of any moth that hovers to feed at the flower. The stigma is bent downwards. The wings and head of moths visiting flowers at this stage become dusted with pollen but, because it's bent down, don't touch the stigma.

During the following day, each flower in the cluster becomes more yellow in colour, its petal tube bends slightly downwards, and the stigma bends upwards. On the second and subsequent evenings, the wings and head of visiting moths touch the stigma and so transfer any pollen they're carrying. To ensure they continue to visit, the scent and the production of nectar continue for several days.

In other words, each flower is functionally male when it first opens but then becomes functionally female. Since the flowers don't all open at the same time, different flowers are at different stages and cross-pollination can occur. Its effectiveness can be seen by the way clusters of sticky, bright-red berries develop from the old flowers.

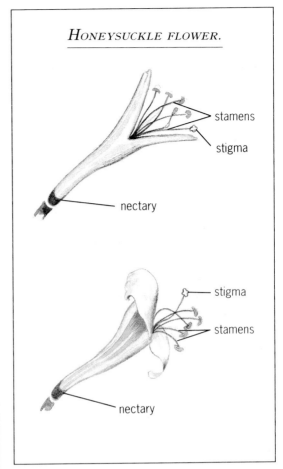

HONEYSUCKLE FLOWER.

stamens

stigma

nectary

stigma

stamens

nectary

*Honeysuckle flower shown at two different stages: newly opened (**above**) and when older (**below**).*

NECTAR THIEVES

Nectar is really there as a bait and a reward for pollinating insects. But sometimes it's taken illegally. This happens when insects find a short cut to the nectar rather than entering the flower in the conventional way.

The short-tongued bees, like the buff-tailed bumble-bee, are often the worst offenders, using their strong jaws to bite holes in the base of flowers to steal nectar, rather than entering legitimately when their short tongues wouldn't reach the nectar anyway.

This is the cause of one of the gardener's perennial problems – runner bean plants that flower well but set little seed. The short-tongued bees bite into the back of the flowers to steal the nectar. So not only do they not pollinate the flowers but, in removing the nectar, they also put off the legitimate visitors. A natural and common garden 'crime' that means no beans for the gardener.

Above, *a long-tongued bumble-bee* Bombus hortorum *feeding at the deep petal tubes of red clover.*

Below, *a buff-tailed bumble-bee, which has a short tongue, steals nectar from a comfrey flower.*

Insects are sure to visit and re-fuel in a garden that is as gaudy and well-advertised as a motorway petrol station, ensuring pollination.

Butterflies, too, may be nectar thieves because they're remarkably opportunist in their feeding. Cabbage whites, in particular, feed at the yellow flowers of cabbage or broccoli that have 'bolted'. The flowers at the bottom of a spike open first and the butterflies approach these in the conventional way from the front and, in so doing, pollinate them. However, they'll then move on to the unopened flowerbuds further up the flower spike and switch to a side approach, inserting their long tongues between the bases of the petals to reach the nectaries. So the plant's cheated because flowers robbed of their nectar don't get pollinated. Alas, there's not much we can do about it.

ENSURING POLLINATION

It's obviously in the gardener's interest, particularly if fruiting crops are grown, to do everything possible to encourage pollination.

Few garden crops are wind pollinated but sweetcorn is a notable exception. Always plant it in blocks rather than rows, and never singly, so that you maximise the chance of pollen being blown on to the stigmas of different plants. Complete pollination will result in full cobs.

Ensuring insect pollination is more difficult but you can increase your chances by increasing the numbers of insects visiting and pollinating fruiting plants or those you want to collect seed from.

The first step is to make your garden a place that bees and other insects regularly visit, and you can do this by planting a colourful and fragrant mixture of flowers, even in a vegetable garden, so that the garden is as gaudy and well-advertised as a motorway petrol station. That way, you make it highly likely that insects will drop

in to 'refuel'.

If your garden's in an exposed, windy position you'll have problems with pollination because insects are blown away and have difficulty alighting on flowers or hovering in front of them. The remedy is to plant a shelter-belt of shrubs and trees on the windward side of the plants. Insects will then visit and remain longer.

And it goes without saying that you must *never* spray with pesticides. Bumble-bees in particular are very susceptible and, though some pesticides are better than others, all are more or less indiscriminate in what they kill.

COMPATIBILITY

Most fruit trees, especially apples and pears, are not self-fertile so pollen has to be provided by another tree of a different variety. That means you need to grow two varieties that flower at the same time and are capable of pollinating each other. You can leave the rest to the insects.

There are so many enjoyable varieties of apples that it may be a hard task to decide which pair or group you want to grow. The main thing to look for is two that flower at the same time, though there are exceptions. Some varieties simply won't pollinate other apples so, if you want to grow Bramley's Seedling, for example, you'll need three varieties. If you have space for a group of trees, plant something like Fiesta, Discovery, Spartan and the cooker, Bramley's Seedling, and you'll have no pollination problems.

If you have space for only one apple tree, you can ensure pollination by planting a flowering crab-apple, like *Malus* 'Golden Hornet', which will also give a magnificent display of white flowers and bright yellow crab-apples. Alternatively, it's possible to buy a 'family tree' with three varieties grafted on the same tree.

It's also likely, of course, that your neighbour's garden will have an apple tree close enough to pollinate yours.

Pears are slightly more difficult to grow than apples and it's less likely that your neighbours will have trees to help pollinate yours. They also need cross-pollinating so choose your varieties carefully. Conference is a favourite variety and is sometimes self-pollinated but much better fruits result from cross-pollination. If you plant a selection from Conference, Onward, Louise Bonne of Jersey, Williams' Bon Chrétien and Doyenné du Comice, you'll be assured of good pollination.

Some plums and cherries also need a pollinator, though not all so it's possible to manage with just one tree. Victoria, Czar, Denniston's Superb, Marjorie's Seedling and most damsons are self-fertile plums, while Stella and Morello (cooking) are self-fertile cherries. Apricots, nectarines and peaches are self-fertile, although you may have to ensure seed set by hand-pollination (see page 125).

There's a special problem with trees that bear male and female flowers on different plants. Holly, for example, is grown for its autumn and winter show of bright berries but it often disappoints. If you want berries you need a female tree, and a male to provide pollen: bear in mind that the chances of getting a male and a female tree are better if you buy three trees rather than just two! Fortunately, however, there are some varieties, like 'J.C. van Tol' that are self-fertile so only one plant is needed.

Some people prefer the patterned leaves of variegated hollies and here, whoever named the popular varieties was obviously having a bad day! Golden Queen is a male-only variety so never bears berries, although

it will pollinate the variety Golden King which, confusingly, is female. Variegated hollies are only varieties of normal holly, not a different species, so female trees are pollinated by ordinary holly and *vice versa*.

Pollination of tomatoes may sometimes be a problem in greenhouses because the air and plants are still and there may be few, if any, pollinating insects. Shaking the plants or spraying the flowers with water every morning moves the pollen from flower to flower and ensures a good crop.

HAND-POLLINATION

Peach, apricot and nectarine flowers are self-fertile but flower early in the year, often before there are many pollinating insects around. So, you have to become the bumble-bee yourself by going round the trees with a soft paint-brush and gently dabbing it into each open flower to brush the pollen on to each stigma.

If the weather's cold for insects when your apple and pear trees flower, you could also try hand-pollination of these with a paint-brush, although in this instance you'll need to transfer pollen from a tree of a different variety.

This is exactly the process used by commercial seed-growers when they're producing 'F1 hybrids'. The job has to be done every time seed is required which is why it's so expensive.

Marrows, courgettes, squashes and pumpkins are borne on plants that have separate male and female flowers, and it's only the female flowers that set fruit. If the weather's cold and wet when they flower, and there are few pollinating insects around, it may be necessary to ensure fruit set by hand-pollinating the female flowers. You can recognise them by the small swelling of an embryo fruit behind the petals. Do the

HAND-POLLINATING FEMALE MARROW FLOWERS.

female flower

male flower

female flower

*Hand-pollinating female marrow flowers: using an entire male flower with its petals folded back (**above left**) and by transferring pollen from a male flower using a soft paintbrush (**above right**).*

pollinating on a warm, sunny day if possible, when both male and female flowers are fully open. Remove a male flower, fold back its petals and dab the pollen laden stamens over the stigma of three or four female flowers. Alternatively, like the peach, you can use a soft paint-brush to transfer pollen from male to female flowers. It may be necessary to go on doing this for several days or until the weather's suitable for pollinating insects to visit. When insect pollinators are around they'll efficiently and successfully pollinate all the female flowers and save you the trouble.

Older varieties of greenhouse cucumber pose a different problem. With varieties like 'Telegraph' male flowers have to be removed as soon as they open. If female flowers are pollinated, the resulting fruits will be bitter and swollen with seeds. Fortunately, breeders have come to our aid with newer varieties that produce only female flowers,

Holly berries are produced on female trees but a male tree is necessary for pollination.

Most sorts of apple trees are not self-fertile, so you need to grow two varieties that flower at the same time. Insects will transfer pollen from one to the other.

so it's best to stick to those.

Outdoor cucumbers, however, must be pollinated if fruits are to develop, so don't remove male flowers from these, and if the weather's poor and there are few pollinating insects around, you may have to hand-pollinate as for marrows and squashes.

If, as gardeners, we are literally to enjoy the fruits of our labours, pollination is essential, whether it be achieved by the agency of wind, insects, or of ourselves wielding a paint-brush.

CHAPTER SEVEN

PESTS – THE BANE OF GARDENERS

There's one fact we gardeners may as well come to terms with straightaway. Whatever we do, we have only part ownership of our gardens and, like it or not, we share them with other wildlife.

While many garden visitors, like the birds, the bees and the hedgehogs, will almost certainly be welcomed some are herbivores, feeding on our prized plants, and that marks them out as 'pests'. Well, we all know what to do with those!

Over the last fifty years or so, we gardeners have faithfully followed the methods of the farmer and blasted with noxious chemicals everything that has the temerity to take a nick out of a lettuce or make a hole in a cabbage leaf. It's certainly not a natural method but it works. Or does it?

It's a sobering thought that in the past fifty years, since we've been using chemical pesticides extensively, pest problems have actually got *worse*. This is partly because the constant use of one chemical tends to

result in the emergence of a resistant strain of the pest so that chemical has to be replaced by another, often stronger, one and so it goes on.

Furthermore, pesticides are indiscriminate in their action though some are better than others. Usually what kills greenfly kills hoverflies too and what wipes out slugs kills the friendly groundbeetles. By destroying our friends and the pests' enemies we're upsetting the natural balance and digging an ever deeper hole for ourselves.

With no natural enemies, pests increase at a much faster rate so, what starts as a minor infestation rapidly builds up, necessitating major chemical warfare.

Even the so-called 'organic' pesticides kill everything they touch so it's much more sensible to rely on nature's own methods. It's far better for wildlife and the environment, and because it makes for a more pleasant, living garden, it's better for the gardener too. Above all, it works better.

GARDEN PESTS

Some of the more troublesome garden pests. In varied gardens, they are effectively controlled by predators.

A ROLL-CALL OF GARDEN HERBIVORES

Greenfly and blackfly

Greenfly and blackfly (properly called aphids) are traditionally the bane of gardeners' lives. There always seem to be so many of them! They damage plants because of their feeding method and, when they build up to large numbers, can cause considerable havoc. They stick their slender, pointed mouthparts through plant tissues and into the sugar-carrying vessels, from which they constantly suck sugars and other nutrients.

What they're really after are nitrogen-containing substances that are used to build proteins. But these are carried in only minute amounts in the sugar-transporting vessels so the aphids take on board copious quantities of sugary fluid, and excrete the excess sugar as honeydew. That's why the ground beneath aphid-infested plants (and cars parked under aphid-infested trees) becomes spattered with sticky sugar on which there often grows an unsightly black mould.

Aphids deprive plants of food because they extract so much sugar and, equally seriously, they're responsible for transmitting virus diseases from one plant to another. No gardener welcomes their presence.

There are many different sorts of aphids, most confined to just one foodplant. However, a few, including the notorious blackfly of beans, spend part of the year on different plants, such as spindle, mock orange (*Philadelphus*) and *Viburnum* in the case of bean blackfly aphids. It's very difficult to rid your plants of blackfly if you also grow one of their other foodplants because there's a fresh infestation every summer.

Aphids reproduce at a fantastic rate, often by virgin birth, and almost all those on your beans will be females, each of which already contains tiny daughters waiting to be born. That's why numbers build up so rapidly.

Spittlebugs

You'll almost certainly have seen 'cuckoo-spit' on a variety of plants and this is caused by spittlebugs. They feed in a similar way to aphids, although their feeding tubes are inserted into the water-carrying vessels of plants. Each blob of cuckoo-spit contains a tiny, green spittlebug nymph which will eventually grow and develop into a brownish frog-hopper.

Their food, like that of aphids, is very dilute, but in this case their problem is excess water. As they excrete the water they pump air into it, forming the characteristic cuckoo-spit, which has a protective function. It stops the vulnerable little nymph from drying out and also conceals it from birds and other predators. There's no doubt that they're a drain on plants, but they're never so abundant as aphids so they do less harm.

They also differ from aphids in being less fussy feeders. The same common species sucks fluids from more than 150 sorts of plants, as different from each other as ferns, lilies, poplar trees and rosemary.

Whitefly

Whitefly also feed in a similar way, although in this case the targets are individual cells. The real culprits are the tiny, scale-like young, which are almost immobile, while the adults look like minute white moths and rise in clouds from infested cabbages. The cabbage whitefly, often so abundant as to make brassicas just about inedible and certainly unpalatable, is a different species from the greenhouse whitefly which attacks cucumbers, tomatoes, aubergines and such indoor plants. They can be dealt with easily and effectively in the greenhouse by biological control using a small parasitic wasp (see page 147).

Caterpillars

Caterpillars of moths and butterflies feed voraciously by chewing plants with massive, hard jaws. Few butterflies, other than the all too common cabbage whites, cause problems for the gardener but a range of moths have caterpillars that eat garden plants.

The caterpillars of many species of common garden moths are wide-ranging feeders. Those of the so-called cabbage moth, for instance, and of the dot moth each feed on at least 38 different sorts of plants. But other moths are more restricted, sometimes feeding upon just a single species.

Some moth caterpillars are known as cutworms. They live in the soil and chew through the roots and lower stems of plants, especially tender ones, so that they wilt, topple over and die.

Sawflies

Sawfly larvae look and behave like caterpillars but have more legs. Several sorts may be abundant in gardens, including the gooseberry sawfly and the Solomon's seal sawfly, which can rapidly defoliate their host plants.

Sawflies are related to bees and wasps but lack a 'waist'. Their name derives from the saw-edged egg-tube which females use to cut slits in stems and leaves for their eggs.

Apart from those particular sawflies mentioned, they don't do much damage.

Beetles

Some beetles cause quite bad damage to specific plants. Leaf beetles chew away at the leaves of garden plants and their larvae often eat the roots as well. The red lily beetle and the orange and black asparagus beetle strip leaves from their food plants.

Small round holes in leaves of brassicas and other plants show where flea beetles have been at work, and young brassica plants may be severely damaged.

Weevils, recognisable by their prominent 'snouts' are also beetles, and they too feed on leaves, while their legless larvae eat roots, stems and seeds. The worst by far are the vine weevils. The adult feeds on a variety of garden plants, leaving notches around the edges of leaves. Far more damaging are the larvae which eat the roots of almost any plant.

A number of other beetles sometimes rank as pests. Wireworms, the larvae of click beetles, attack the roots of potatoes and other plants, while the fat, white larvae of cockchafers feed extensively on plant roots.

Flies

The developing larvae of a variety of flies cause great problems. What vegetable-grower has not been troubled by the grubs of cabbage root fly, carrot fly and onion fly?

Of course, there are other insects that are herbivores but they rarely cause real problems, so they can't really be classified as pests. Only aphids, caterpillars, sawfly larvae, leaf beetles, a few flies and weevils cause real problems. But there are other plant-eaters in gardens!

*Black bean aphids (**above**) spend part of the year on spindle, mock orange and Viburnum, but in summer move on to beans (**left**), and many other plants. They reproduce at a fantastic rate, usually by virgin birth.*
***Below**, false-colour electron micrograph of wingless female aphids feeding. The needle-like mouthparts inserted into the stem are visible on the aphid to the right.*
***Opposite**, Lily beetles attack lilies.*
***Opposite below**, Large white butterfly caterpillars hatching from eggs.*

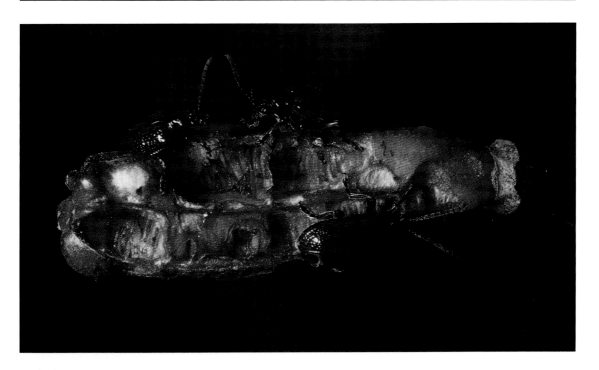

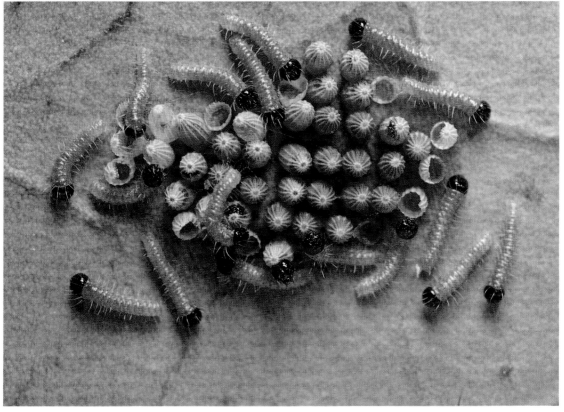

Slugs and snails

Slugs and snails are a constant thorn in every gardener's flesh. They're super-abundant and they have an extremely efficient way of eating plant tissues. Attached to the floor of their mouths is a continuously-growing 'conveyor belt' of tiny, jagged teeth, which bite against a horny jaw in the roof of the mouth. This apparatus rapidly and destructively rasps away at plant tissue and conveys it back down the throat. Unlike most animals, slugs and snails can digest the cellulose that forms the bulk of plant tissue so they make the most of their food.

MIXED PLANTING

Before any herbivore can eat and damage your plants, it has to find them. Most use one or other (sometimes both) of two senses – sight and smell. Cabbage aphids, for instance, recognise Brussels sprout plants by their characteristic silhouette so they find them more easily when they're surrounded by bare soil. As good a reason for letting the weeds flourish, as ever there was!

Cabbage white butterflies and flea beetles, however, locate their foodplants by their characteristic odour, and it's a fair bet that moths and other insects do the same. Cabbages give out an unmistakable odour caused by the chemical sinigrin and its mustard oil products. What better advertisement to a cabbage white than a whole field of 'smelly' cabbages or other brassicas.

The main smell receptors of insects are on their antennae but, once attracted to the cabbage plant, other receptors on the feet and mouthparts come into play. If the combination of smell, touch and taste is right, the insect proceeds to feed or to lay its eggs.

Ironically, the chemical substances that give particular plants their characteristic odour and taste were evolved by plants as defences against insect attack. They're meant to make the plant smell and taste different and unsuitable as food. But many insects now use that odour as a label for recognising and identifying their particular foodplant. Sometimes, as happens with aromatic plants, we too can smell the chemicals involved but insects' chemical senses are much more finely tuned than ours and they detect and recognise minute concentrations of many chemicals.

Both methods that insects use to find their foodplants, sight and smell, can be foiled by confusing them. It's hardly surprising that a cabbage white can locate and respond to a field of cabbages and their undiluted smell but if you present them with a mixed array of odours this will disorient and confuse them. So don't plant your cabbages in large blocks but interplant them with ornamentals, herbs or some other vegetable – the more aromatic, the better. Tomatoes, onions, sweet basil and French marigolds, for instance, grown among the cabbages will tend to deter the cabbage-eating pests.

Such mixed planting has a long pedigree. It is used in traditional cottage gardens, by peasant farmers throughout the tropics, was practised in monastery gardens, and you can still see it in the restored Renaissance gardens of the Château de Villandry in the Loire Valley. Companion planting enthusiasts will tell you that some plant associations are mutually beneficial because the plants 'grow better' together but the more reasonable explanation is that mixed planting deters insect pests or attracts their natural predators (see page 142).

Mixed planting will also help deter or confuse those insects that locate their foodplants by sight. The characteristic silhouettes and shapes of particular plants will be hidden or disguised by surrounding plants.

Interplanting with flowers or another crop is one possibility but another is to allow some growth of weeds. Obviously you don't want rampant weeds that would compete with your crop for light, water or nutrients but a low covering of green around cultivated plants is no bad thing, and certainly preferable to bare soil. Good ground cover in the vegetable patch has additional advantages in that it shelters natural predators of pests (see page 142).

A ROLL-CALL OF GARDEN PREDATORS

There would seem to be unlimited food for plant-eaters in gardens but most are pretty choosy about what they eat, both with regard to species and to quality. It's obvious, too, that there's usually some natural check on numbers because pests rarely get completely out of control. This is partly because nearly all of them have enemies of their own. As in any natural environment there are many small-scale dramas happening daily in the garden as the predatory animal-eaters tackle the plant-eaters. The numbers of each species of predator are never anything like as high as the numbers of each species of plant-eater but there are many more different sorts.

Wasps

The yellow and black wasps that so often plague your meals in the garden, and which can give a painful sting, are terrific predators. There are two common species, the so-called common wasp and the German wasp, and five rarer ones including the large hornet.

They're all social species, a nest being started in spring by an over-wintered queen, which raises a brood of infertile, female workers who then take over all the duties of the nest other than egg-laying, which is the queen's task.

Workers are produced throughout the summer until, in autumn, a brood of males and virgin queens emerge. They leave the nest, mating takes place and the nest society gradually breaks down. Workers, males and the old queen then die, and only newly-impregnated queens survive the winter to start the cycle again. The nests are constructed of wood fibres chewed into 'paper'. They're impressive structures, about the size of a football in the case of common and German wasps, but they're used for only one year.

Adult wasps feed on nectar and other sweet fluids but they also catch animal food to feed to their developing grubs in the nest. Caterpillars, sawfly larvae and any reasonably soft-bodied insects are hunted down, captured, and chewed into 'insect hamburger', pellets of which are taken back to the nest for the grubs.

A large wasp nest in a garden may be a nuisance or a hazard, particularly with regard to the safety of young children or the elderly, but if you can bear to keep it, the wasps will make massive inroads on the caterpillars and other herbivores in the garden.

Other garden wasps, and there are many different sorts, are solitary species. A female constructs a few cells in a secluded place, such as a hollow stem, stocks each with animal food (usually paralysed by stinging), and lays an egg on the food in each cell. The resulting larva eats the stored food, pupates, and emerges as an adult the

Fields of cabbages act like a magnet to cabbage white butterflies because of their strong smell.

The 'paper' nests of common wasps become as large as footballs and produce about 12,000 wasps.

Mixed planting of flowers and vegetables tends to confuse and disorient potential pests.

In a traditional cottage garden there are few pest problems because of mixed planting and natural control.

following year, having had no contact with its mother. Different species stock their little nests with different sorts of prey. Some use caterpillars, some aphids, some flies including hoverflies, some spiders and so on. Inevitably, some beneficial insects get killed but, on balance, solitary wasps consume many more pests.

The vast majority of wasps are parasitic and many are tiny; these include ichneumons, chalcids and braconids. Females lay their eggs on or in other sorts of insects or spiders, and each egg hatches into a larva which gradually eats its host before pupating and eventually turning into an adult wasp.

Most sorts of insect in the garden are parasitised by one or more species of these wasps, parasites of caterpillars, sawflies, hoverflies and other flies, aphids, lacewings and spiders being particularly common. Beneficial insects as well as pests are destroyed but, on the whole, the parasitic wasps do a good job for the gardener in controlling troublesome plant-eaters.

Hoverfly larvae

Amongst the most voracious predators of aphids are the larvae of many species of hoverflies. Adult females are attracted to clusters of aphids, among which they lay their eggs, not in batches but singly so that each has plenty of food. They hatch into rather flattened green, brown or whitish, legless larvae, each of which may eat several hundred aphids during the course of its growth and development. A hoverfly larva may look sluggish but it can move with astonishing speed to seize an aphid in its arrow-shaped mouthparts. It raises the aphid aloft, sucks out all the fluids and finally discards, husk-like, an empty skin. It's not unusual to find once-infested cabbage plants completely clean of aphids but dotted with pear-shaped hoverfly pupae. It's only the larvae which eat aphids, the adults feed on nectar and other sweet fluids and on pollen.

Lacewings

Lacewings are delicate-looking brown or green insects. Their wings are densely netted with veins and are held roof-like over the body when at rest. Some species lay their eggs directly on to plants but others have bizarre-looking eggs on stalks. They hatch into spindle-shaped greyish or greenish insects with three pairs of legs and they're hungry eaters of aphids, mites and other small animals. They have sickle-shaped, tubular jaws with which they grasp their prey and suck out the juices. Strangely, some larvae decorate and camouflage their bodies with the drained skins of their prey. Adult lacewings are mostly fluid-feeders but they have jaws and some occasionally eat aphids.

Ladybirds

Most sorts of ladybirds and their larvae eat aphids and other small animals, which they crunch up with their powerful jaws. Everyone recognises an adult ladybird but their agile, splay-legged larvae are perhaps less familiar. They're grey or blackish, ornamented with pale yellow or orange spots. When fully grown, each hunches over and becomes a rather blob-like pupa, from which the adult ladybird emerges.

There are several species of ladybirds in gardens, the commonest being the red and black 2-spot and 7-spot, and the black and yellow 14-spot. The tiny, black-spotted, yellow 22-spot feeds on mildew rather than other insects.

Ground beetles

Fast-moving black or dark brown ground beetles are usually seen scuttling away under a stone or overhanging vegetation. They look a bit evil but you should never put your foot on one because most are at least partly predatory, and their whitish, six-legged larvae, usually found in the soil, always are. Adults and larvae have strong jaws and make short work of any small insect or other animal they catch. Larvae usually hunt over the ground, often in the soil, but the active adults roam freely under cover of darkness, even climbing plants in search of prey.

Many eat springtails and other such small, ground-dwelling insects; others eat caterpillars and anything else they can catch; and some feed on slugs and snails. Not a great deal is known about the diet of ground beetles but they undoubtedly eat a lot of garden pests.

Ants

No garden is without ants, usually the little garden black ant and, occasionally, small yellow ones. Gardeners resent them mainly because they bite through roots when constructing their nests but it should never be forgotten that they're efficient and high-powered predators which tackle, by sheer weight of numbers, prey much larger than themselves. True, they tend to protect aphids in exchange for sweet honeydew, but they also catch and eat many other garden pests.

Spiders

Perhaps the most fearsome and effective predators in gardens are spiders. They're present in considerable numbers and great variety, some small, others quite large, and they're found on the ground, on tree-trunks and fences, and on plants. Many use silken snares of one sort or another to trap and tangle their prey but others are mobile hunters. Most deliver a bite that poisons their prey. The spider injects digestive enzymes into its victim, which means that it can then suck out a pre-digested 'soup', for spiders have only tiny mouths. It's probably true to say that a spider will eat any animal it can overpower, including other spiders, so they're useful garden predators.

Centipedes

Fast-moving brown centipedes are also useful predators. They hunt mainly at ground level but it is probable that they also sometimes climb plants at night. Just behind the mouth is a pair of poison claws which grasps and paralyses or kills prey before it's chewed up by the powerful jaws. Centipedes, like spiders and ants, are almost certainly general predators tackling anything they can catch and overcome.

Larger animals

It's not only the smaller animals that help us gardeners with pest control. Many of the commoner garden birds are very effective predators too. Blue-tits, great-tits, wrens, robins and other small birds eat aphids, small caterpillars and other garden insects. Blackbirds feed avidly on caterpillars, even the supposedly distasteful yellow and black caterpillars of large white butterflies. Starlings probe lawns for leather-jackets, cutworms and other insect food, and song thrushes make a speciality of snails, whose shells they smash on 'anvil-stones'.

Even the seed-eating birds like greenfinches and chaffinches collect insects to feed to their nestlings, and the swifts and

GARDEN PREDATORS

Some of the predators that exercise control over pests in gardens.

Cabbage aphids and two hoverfly larvae, which eat aphids by sucking them dry with their arrow-shaped mouthparts.

Adults of the hoverfly larvae shown on the left. Marigolds near your cabbages will attract them to lay eggs.

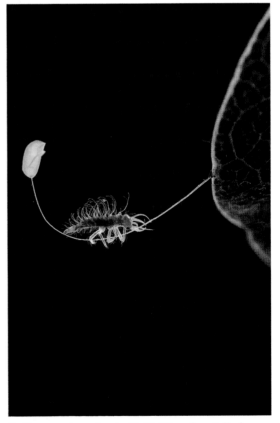

Left, *green lacewing in flight. These lay stalked eggs beneath leaves.*

Above, *the newly-hatched larva climbs along the egg stalk to start catching and eating aphids.*

house martins, circling in the air above the garden, snap up all the winged aphids and other airborne insects they encounter. Of course, insect-eating birds inevitably take beneficial insects as well but, on balance, they play a major role in controlling pests.

Frogs, toads and newts pass long periods of their adult life away from the ponds in which they were bred. On land their diet is varied, including beetles, caterpillars, flies, snails and slugs, so building a pond in your garden helps greatly with pest control.

Slugs are perhaps the most troublesome garden pest. They're present in enormous numbers and not many animals eat them. All the more reason then to encourage our good friend the hedgehog. Hedgehogs have a very varied diet and will eat just about any animal they can get hold of. If you're lucky enough to enjoy visits from hedgehogs, take care of them by leaving heaps of dead leaves and brushwood undisturbed as hibernation sites and always check for hedgehogs before setting fire to bonfires in autumn and winter. Don't give them bread and milk because cows' milk gives them diarrhoea. Tinned dog food is better, though if they become too well fed on that they'll have little incentive to hunt out slugs.

ATTRACTING AND ENCOURAGING PREDATORS

There are few predators that we can specifically attract into our gardens but we can go a long way towards ensuring that we have hoverfly larvae. Female hoverflies need a meal of pollen before they lay their eggs but they have short tongues and cannot cope with deep flowers. So planting open, accessible flowers near to aphid-prone plants increases the chances that females will feed and then lay their eggs amongst the aphids.

Use plants like English marigolds (*Calendula*), French marigolds (*Tagetes patula*), single asters (*Callistephus chinensis*), and black-eyed susan (*Rudbeckia hirta*), poppies, dwarf convolvulus (*Convolvulus minor*) and, especially, the poached egg flower (*Limnanthes douglasii*). Generally, a wide diversity of planting will not only attract many more insects but will also help to deter pests (see page 134).

A pond is a must since all insects and larger animals need a drink from time to time and, of course, you'll attract frogs, toads and newts.

Trees, shrubs and climbers of varying heights will tempt more birds to nest. Providing nest-boxes also helps, though you should avoid overdoing them or you may end up with more birds than the garden can provide food for, resulting in mass starvation of the little nestlings. Also be careful to site nest-boxes well out of the way of cats.

All garden predators will benefit from planting a good variety of plants and also increasing the structural diversity. Make sure there are plants of different heights and structure, giving a complex mosaic of open, sunny places and dense shade. Variety is the key if your garden is to be rich in animal life, including all the predators that naturally hold pests in check.

Ground beetles, centipedes and spiders will benefit enormously if you maintain good ground cover, whether by intentional planting or by tolerating non-competitive weeds. By day they shelter from their own predators – the birds – beneath low plants, but at night they roam about and over the plants looking for food. So that's another reason for interplanting vegetable crops with decorative plants to cover bare soil. Ground-hugging plants such as creeping Jenny (*Lysimachia nummularia*) and spotted dead-nettle (*Lamium maculatum*) are invaluable for supplying good ground cover.

Maintaining a rich, well-balanced garden should mean that you avoid most pest problems but there are a few specific controls for particular pests. Cutworms, chafers, leather-jackets and wireworms can be dealt with by hoeing the soil around the bases of plants to expose them to view – the birds will do the rest.

Carrot flies, when looking for somewhere to lay their eggs, fly a few centimetres above the ground. A polythene barrier on short posts erected around carrots will deflect the pests up and away from your crop. A covering of very fine netting over any crop subject to attack by flying insects will provide complete protection.

Cabbage root flies lay their eggs in the soil right next to the plant. The solution is to surround the stem at soil level with foam-rubber carpet underlay, so that they can't get to the soil. A 15 cm (6 in) square of underlay with a slit in to the centre and a small cross-slit at the centre can be eased around the base of each cabbage plant and will always do the trick.

One way or another, all pest populations can be kept at acceptable levels but don't expect to get rid of them all completely. If that happened, the predators would also die out because of lack of food and the garden would become as sterile and dead as one that has been sprayed with chemicals.

Surround the plants with a polythene barrier as soon as the carrots are planted out. Carrot flies fly a few centimetres above the ground and when they meet the barrier will fly upwards and miss the crop.

Cut a piece of foam rubber carpet underlay into 15 cm (6 in) squares, make a slit into the centre of each and a small cross-slit at the centre. Slip each piece of underlay around the base of a plant, ensuring that it fits tightly. This keeps female flies away from the soil next to the roots, where they lay eggs.

DEFENCE AGAINST CARROT FLY.

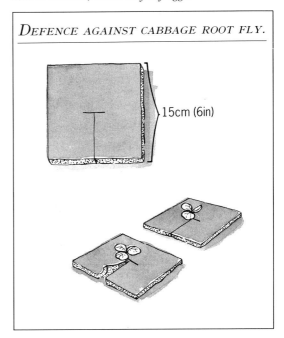

DEFENCE AGAINST CABBAGE ROOT FLY.

15cm (6in)

Toads spend most of their time on land, catching and eating insects and other invertebrates.

Black-eyed Susan Rudbeckia hirta *attracts feeding hoverflies which then lay eggs among aphids.*

A garden that is structurally varied gives shelter to many animals including valuable predators.

CHAPTER EIGHT

MANIPULATING NATURE

These days nobody needs reminding that we meddle with nature at our peril. Most of us have come to realise that we don't *own* the natural world, we're simply a small part of it and it's incumbent on us to conserve it. But, of course, the fact remains that we're part of the amazing, complex chain of life and that entitles us to use our own evolutionary advantage – our intelligence.

If we're to use this wisely, to create real, long-term and sustainable advantages for our species, it must be employed not to fight natural forces but to help them along. There's no more graphic illustration of the wisdom of co-operating with nature than in the garden. Every single tool that we've ever needed to produce beautiful gardens and bumper harvests is there, created by nature and willingly loaned to us. We just need the common sense to use them.

BIOLOGICAL CONTROL

The control of pests by harnessing natural processes has been around a long time. For centuries, the Chinese have encouraged ants to control pests of citrus fruits, and Victorian gardeners often kept a toad in the greenhouse to deal with insects. But biological control has come a long way since then.

It really got off the ground in 1888, when a ladybird from Australia was successfully introduced to Californian citrus orchards to control cotton 'cushiony scale'. Since then countless attempts, some successful, some not, have been made to control pests by introducing predators, parasites or diseases.

The Australians had great success in controlling the prickly pear cactus, which was taking over enormous areas of Queensland, by introducing a moth whose caterpillars eat the cactus.

Pests in the garden in Britain are actually quite easy to keep under control by encouraging the predators that also live in the garden (see chapter 7). The greenhouse is different. It's an enclosed environment, often kept artificially warm, and it lacks predators.

But now, because commercial growers have started to move towards biological methods of control, many predators of common pests have become available to the gardener. All you have to do is to release them into the greenhouse.

The common red spider mite (*Tetranychus urticae*) is so called because the overwintering form, which hides in the greenhouse structure, is brick-red, although the rest of the year it's greenish-yellow. So tiny are they that they're only just visible to the naked eye but they produce silken strands and, when infestation is heavy, plants become shrouded with fine webbing which is quite easy to recognise.

The mites suck sap from leaf cells, causing a mottling of the leaves which eventually become brown and shrivelled. They multiply very rapidly in a hot greenhouse and can cause serious damage before you notice them. The natural predator of red spider mite is another mite, *Phytoseiulus persimilis*. It's slightly larger, orange in colour and fast-moving. Each one will eat about 30 eggs or five adults of red spider mite every day and eventually always eliminates them.

As soon as you find red spider mite (you may need to search closely, usually with a hand lens), order *Phytoseiulus* from a supplier (see addresses on page 213) and make sure you tell them the size of your greenhouse and the seriousness of the infestation. You'll receive bean leaves bearing the predator and also, of course, a few red spider mites as food. Distribute the leaves evenly around the greenhouse (cut them up if necessary), putting a piece on each infected plant, and leave them for at least a week so that any eggs hatch. Predatory mites quickly move on to your plants and start feeding so within two to six weeks the spider mites should have disappeared.

Of course, without food, the predators will also eventually die out so, if you have further trouble, you'll have to buy in more. The mites work best at 25°C (77°F) and the temperature should not fall below 13°C (55°F).

You can't miss greenhouse whitefly (*Trialeurodes vaporariorum*). The adults cluster on the undersides of leaves like hundreds of miniature white moths and their eggs hatch into minute larvae which disperse before feeding and become flat, immobile 'scales'. These, too, feed on cell sap, so that leaves turn yellow and die, and they also excrete sugary honeydew which makes leaves sticky and often smothered with an unsightly black mould. Whitefly can survive even freezing conditions for about a month so they may survive winter outside the greenhouse, to re-infest the plants the following spring.

The predator for these is a tiny parasitic wasp, *Encarsia formosa*, most of which are female. Each lays about 50 eggs in different whitefly scales. The eggs hatch into larvae which eat the developing whitefly, eventually turning each scale black.

About three weeks after the eggs are laid, an adult wasp emerges from each parasitised scale and flies straight towards whitefly, attracted by their smell. While the parasite's life-cycle takes about three weeks at 25°C (77°F), it takes up to ten weeks at 15°C (59°F), so control is better in a really warm greenhouse.

When you send for *Encarsia*, you'll receive black (that is, parasitised) whitefly scales on a fresh tobacco leaf. Cut it into pieces and hang one bit on each infected plant, but out of direct sunlight. Sometimes bits of tobacco leaf are stuck on to pieces of card which you then hang on the plants. Most parasites will quickly emerge but leave them for three weeks to be on the safe side. In

Biological control by introduced predators is possible in the closed, controlled environment of a greenhouse.

A predatory mite Phytoseiulus persimilis *attacks a plant-feeding red spider mite. They eventually eliminate infestations.*

Heavy infestations of red spider mite Tetranychus urticae *shroud plants in fine silk webbing.*

two to five weeks, depending on temperature, you should begin to find blackened (parasitised) scales on the undersides of leaves on your plants, and these will steadily become more frequent. Ideally, the temperature should be above 21°C (70°F), to give *Encarsia* every chance to control the whitefly. Under these conditions, about 25 parasites per square metre of greenhouse floor area should get to grips with a small, evenly distributed whitefly population. *Encarsia* doesn't overwinter so you may need to repeat the operation every year, unless you're able to keep up the heat in winter.

The greenhouse or citrus mealybug (*Planococcus citri*) does best in hot, humid greenhouses. There can be up to eight generations a year at 27°C (81°F). The pink bodies of female adults are covered with fine, white wax threads which protect them. They feed by sucking cell sap and they also excrete sugary honeydew.

The predator to use is a black and orange ladybird, *Cryptolaemus montrouzieri*. Adults can munch their way through three mealybugs a day and larvae eat nine a day. Since the ladybirds may live for seven months and each lays about 500 eggs, they're highly effective predators. The ladybird larvae look somewhat like the mealybugs, as they're also covered with white wax strands, but they're about twice as big.

Cryptolaemus is more difficult to mass produce than other biological controls so it's more expensive. It's normally supplied in batches of ten and these need distributing round the greenhouse, at least one per plant, as they search only a relatively small area for food. Until they're established keep the greenhouse closed to stop them flying away and, for best results, keep the temperature at 20°–26° (68–79°F) with a high humidity.

The pupae of *Cryptolaemus* may be mistaken for dead larvae so don't throw these away, just to make sure.

A bacterium, *Bacillus thuringiensis*, is used to control caterpillars, and it can be used in the garden or greenhouse. Once infected with the bacteria, caterpillars immediately stop feeding and ultimately die. The attraction of using the *Bacillus*, as opposed to a chemical pesticide, is that it only affects caterpillars and has no effects on other garden animals (including yourself). You buy *Bacillus thuringiensis* as a powder containing dried spores. Make it up into a solution and spray it like an insecticide.

Remember that with all biological control the pest must be present as food or host before the predator can get established, and once the pest dies out, so will the predator. Another point to remember is that biological control doesn't necessarily completely eradicate a pest but it keeps damage at a tolerable level.

If you've opted for biological control, avoid using chemical pesticides or you'll kill your predator and, above all, be patient.

INSECT LURES

Some insect pests can be trapped by luring them with the female sex attractant, known as a pheromone. Needless to say, only males come to the trap but if enough are caught there are fewer matings and so less egg-laying and fewer pests.

Commercial growers use pheromone traps to monitor pest numbers and then, when they decide that the situation's getting serious, they use a chemical insecticide. This is the case with codling moths, which lay eggs on apples into which the resulting grubs burrow. The traps can also be used in the garden for actual control, giving about

80 per cent success.

The time to take action is when petals begin to fall from the apple flowers. Hang a pheromone trap from one of the lower branches, setting one trap to every five trees. It should catch enough males to reduce greatly the number of eggs laid and fruits damaged.

The trap consists of a roof-like, triangular box of plastic with open ends. Inside, the floor is covered with a sheet of sticky paper on which you put a capsule of the female pheromone.

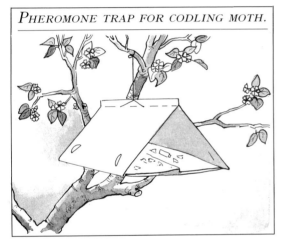

PHEROMONE TRAP FOR CODLING MOTH.

Inside the roof-like, open-ended triangular box of plastic, the floor is covered with a sheet of sticky paper on which is a capsule of the female pheromone.

Similar traps are available to reduce plum sawfly to acceptable levels and there will no doubt be more developments in future.

Research work is continually going on and one possibility being investigated is saturating an area with the female pheromone, so that males are totally confused and can't find the real females. There have also been successful attempts at identifying and synthesising the chemical that attracts a pest to its food, and then using this chemical as a lure in traps. On the other hand repellent chemicals have also been tested (this harks back to the old-fashioned idea of using mothballs to repel cabbage root fly).

A more promising line is the application of a particular insect hormone, called juvenile hormone, which keeps an insect in an immature state, so that it never becomes adult and so never reproduces itself. At present, all these are ideas and possibilities with, as yet, no firm help for the gardener. Who knows, though, what we might be able to do in the future?

PLANT BREEDING

Pests may be relatively easy for the natural gardener to control but diseases are a different matter. All we can do really is to remove infected leaves at the first sign of attack and destroy them. Fortunately, the plant breeders have come to our rescue by producing varieties resistant to many diseases and there are even some that will shrug off pest attacks too.

Different varieties of the same species often show marked variations in resistance to disease. Some roses, for example, are a martyr to blackspot while others will remain free from attack all season. This is because of the variation in the inherited genetic characteristics of each plant. Just as no two fingerprints are alike, so every plant raised from seed is unique. The difference is often so slight as to be more or less unnoticeable but it's always there.

Generally, resistance turns up by sheer chance. An eagle-eyed grower or gardener will notice that while one plant succumbs, a different variety will not, and they're the plants the breeders are looking for.

The breeding process is often rather hit or miss. That resistant variety will be cross-pollinated with others, perhaps of a desirable colour, and the resulting seeds are sown.

Above, *a heavy infestation of whitefly and their larval scales on the underside of a leaf.*

Below, *the little wasp* Encarsia formosa *parasitises whitefly scales by laying an egg in each.*

Three greenhouse mealybugs Planococcus citri *and the predatory ladybird* Cryptolaemus montrouzieri.

The majority will be useless and will be quickly confined to the compost heap but those that retain the resistance may then be further crossed until, eventually, a resistant plant with all the other desirable characteristics is produced.

It can take years to achieve results and, unfortunately, other desirable characteristics may be lost in the process. You may finish up with a rose that's resistant to blackspot with a superb colour but no perfume. Or it may be a weak grower or have a poor flower shape. The permutations are endless.

None the less, breeding for resistance to pests and diseases continues apace and has become the top priority in many cases. There's been much success already. There are potatoes that are resistant to blight, tomatoes that are rarely hit by virus diseases, snapdragons that shrug off rust and phlox that's disliked by eelworms.

If you're raising plants from seed, buy through a catalogue where you'll find much more information on pest and disease resistance; if you're buying fruit plants, go to a specialist; and, if you want disease-free roses, buy a good book or talk to the growers.

Plant breeding has also improved the productivity of many fruits and vegetables and resulted in stronger, more robust flowers that will often stand the weather better too.

The most productive, large-flowering and attractive plants arise from a direct crossing of two varieties. They're called F1 hybrids and have what is known as 'hybrid vigour'. When two plants are crossed for the first time, the resulting seedlings are always more vigorous and sturdy. The symbol 'F1' simply means a first-generation cross. Unfortunately, if you were to collect seed from F1 hybrids the resulting seedlings would be unlike the parent so whenever seed is needed, the original cross has to be made again. That's why the seed's expensive.

Recent and accelerating advances in genetic engineering (where a particular, desirable gene can be transferred from one plant to another, even to a different species), hold out great hopes for the farmer and gardener. It will soon be possible to transfer resistance to pests and diseases by genetic engineering even from, say, a potato to a rose.

The possibilities are endless. Success is already claimed in making plants taste of unexpected things, like fish, but there again perhaps that's not such an attractive idea! Another possibility being pursued is the genetical engineering of pest species so that they no longer have the habits, usually eating habits, that cause the problem.

The fear always aroused is that this is truly 'meddling with nature' and the resulting plants or animals may turn out to be 'monsters' that will wreak unlooked-for-havoc. It's an understandable but almost certainly groundless fear. We shall have to be cautious in the development of the technique.

PRUNING AND TRAINING

There are quite a few plants that we want to alter in shape. Over the generations, gardeners have discovered how to do it, though in the earliest times, it would have been very much a process of trial and error. Now we know much more about plant growth and the hormones involved (see page 91) we can use this knowledge to bend nature's rules a bit and train plants to grow as we want them.

Most plants are naturally fairly bushy with many side shoots and branches but sometimes we don't want that sort of growth. With plants like greenhouse tomatoes, and chrysanthemums or dahlias grown for show, we are aiming for a

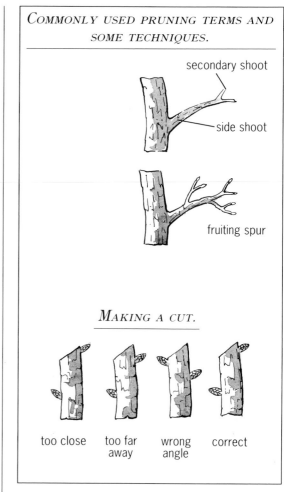

COMMONLY USED PRUNING TERMS AND SOME TECHNIQUES.

secondary shoot

side shoot

fruiting spur

MAKING A CUT.

too close — too far away — wrong angle — correct

Side-shoot. *A shoot arising from the main stem of the plant.*
Secondary shoot. *A shoot arising from a side-shoot.*
Fruiting spur. *A collection of shoots on which the fruit is produced. Made by cutting side-shoots and secondary shoots back hard.*
Leading shoot. *The main stem (or stems) which extends the branch system.*
Downward-facing bud. *Refers to the angle of the bud on the shoot. Buds can also be outward-, inward- and upward-facing. They are used to advantage when training to shape. Bear in mind that a bud grows in the direction it faces.*

A pruning cut should be angled away from the bud, and be made slightly above it. Do not leave too much stem above the bud as this 'snag' will rot. Do not cut too close to the bud.

TRAINING AN ESPALIER.

Plant the trees at least 3.6 m (12 ft) and preferably 4.5 m (15 ft) apart, against a wall or fence strung with wires at 60 cm (2 ft) intervals. Fix wires to a wall with vine-eyes.

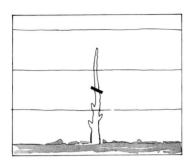

1. Immediately after planting, prune to 5 cm (2 in) above the first wire. (This is 60 cm (2 ft) above the ground.) Make sure there are three good buds below the pruning position.

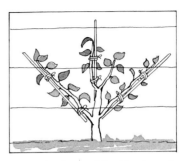

2. In spring, train the resulting shoots on to canes fixed to the wires. Train the side-shoots at an angle of 45 degrees from the main stem.

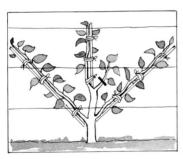

3. In the first summer, cut back any side branches that may have formed on the main stem to 7 cm (3 in).

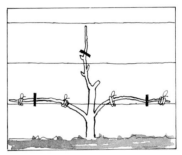

4. In the second winter, tie the two branches that will form the first tier to the lower wire. Prune them back to remove a third of the previous season's growth. Prune the main stem to 5 cm (2 in) above the second wire to encourage three new buds to form the second tier.

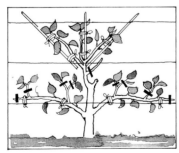

5. In the following summer, prune the side-shoots on the lower two branches to 7 cm (3 in) and secondary shoots to 2.5 cm (1 in). Treat the second tier as you did the first, in the previous summer (see step 3).

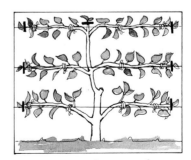

6. Every summer, repeat the process for as many tiers as you wish. At the required height, select out two buds and train these horizontally as the final tier. Thereafter, prune each arm as for cordon training, step 4 (see page 156), pruning in the summer.

reasonable number of large tomatoes and perhaps one giant chrysanthemum or a dahlia bloom on a long, straight stem. It's not difficult to achieve this, by pinching out buds developing in the joints of leaves on the main stem, ending up with an erect, unbranched plant.

On the other hand, some woody shrubs, like the privets used for hedging, are required to put out the maximum number of side shoots so that they thicken out and form a dense screen. We can achieve this by

TRAINING A CORDON.

Cordons should be grown against a post-and-wire support or wires strung at 60 cm (2 ft) intervals on an existing fence. Before planting, tie canes on to the wires to prevent the stems chafing. Plant the trees 75 cm (2 ft 6 in) apart.

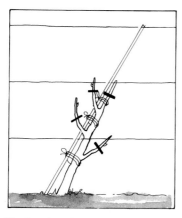

1. Immediately after planting, cut the leading shoot back to remove a third of the growth it made that year. Cut back any side-shoots to a downward-facing bud, leaving each shoot 7 cm (3 in) long.

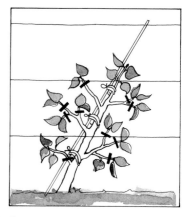

2. In the first summer, prune back side-shoots coming directly from the main stem to 7 cm (3 in). Prune any secondary shoots to 2.5 cm (1 in).

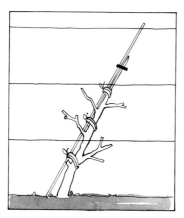

3. In the second winter, prune the leading shoot, cutting off one-third of that year's growth.

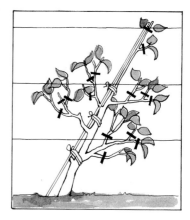

4. Every summer, prune in this way until the end of the cane is reached. Make more room by lowering the cane. When the tree is as long as you want it, prune the main shoot in summer to 7 cm (3 in) and side-shoots to 2.5 cm (1 in).

regularly clipping and pruning shoots, thus removing the apical buds so that their dominance is taken away and lateral buds can develop. So, if you want any plant to become more bushy simply nip out its top bud.

Pruning is a way that we can help nature along by removing dead or diseased wood and old flowering shoots, and opening up the centre of the plant to admit more light and air to promote better growth and flowering.

The main secret when pruning woody plants to encourage strong growth and maximum flowers is to know the type of wood it produces flowers on. Hydrangeas, for example, flower on wood they made the year before so, if you cut the plants hard back at the end of the season, you'll get no

Above, *show chrysanthemums are de-budded to give a single large bloom on each stem.*

Below, *privet hedges are clipped to promote branching and make a thick screen.*

flowers the following year. Obviously, you simply cut out those shoots that have borne a flower and leave the young ones.

Buddleia is quite different because it flowers late in the season on wood it made in the same year. So cut that back really hard in early spring to encourage strong growth and good flowers on the new wood.

Many plants, though, flower on both old and new wood so with them it's just a case of judicious shaping and trimming.

Some, like the brooms, are pruned immediately after flowering just to remove the old flowers. It's a way of dead-heading, preventing the plant using its energies to make seed. And with many plants that grow low and tend to get bare in the middle, like heathers and lavender, it's a good idea to prune with shears just after flowering to remove the seed-making potential and to encourage strong young growth.

In small gardens, most fruit trees are grown trained into cordons, espaliers, fans and the like. The best way to prune these is in the summer when the plants will respond by producing fruit buds rather than the growth buds they would make after winter pruning.

FAN-TRAINING OF PEACHES AND NECTARINES.

This pruning method produces trees that grow flat against a wall. The reflected and stored heat allows otherwise tender fruits to be grown in temperate climates. Grow against wires fixed to a wall 23 cm (9 in) apart.

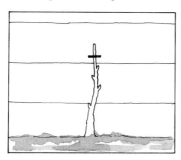

1. Immediately after planting, cut back to a strong bud, making sure there are two buds beneath this. Leave the tree about 45 cm (18 in) high. The following season three shoots will grow.

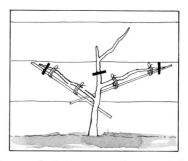

2. In the second winter, remove the central shoot. Prune the two remaining shoots to 45 cm (18 in) long and tie them to canes fixed to the wires about 20 degrees above the horizontal.

3. In the following summer, select four shoots from these side branches; two from the top, one underneath and its extension. Tie them in and rub off any other buds that appear.

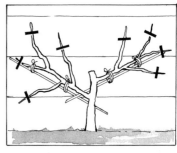

4. In the third winter, cut back the selected shoots, leaving them 45 cm (18 in) long.

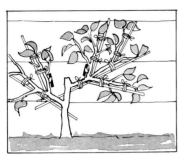

5. *In the following summer, tie in branches as they grow. Select side-shoots 10 cm (4 in) apart to form the fruit-bearing shoots. Rub off any unwanted buds.*

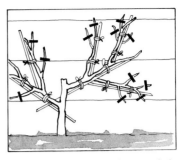

6. *In the fourth winter, reduce the growth from the main framework branches by about half. From now on, pruning is aimed at producing fruit.*

7. *In the following summer, allow the side-shoots to grow four to six leaves and form a new shoot at their base. Pinch out any other new growth.*

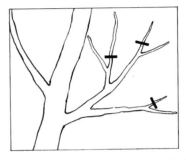

8. *Once the fruit has been picked, prune the fruited shoot out. Tie the replacement shoot into its place. Repeat the process every year.*

TRAINING A DWARF PYRAMID.

Initial pruning establishes the conical shape. After that, all pruning is done in summer to restrict growth. If you are growing more than one, they should be planted 1.5 m (5 ft) apart.

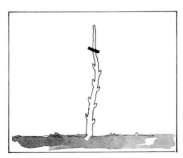

1. *Immediately after planting, cut the stem back to a bud within 60 cm (2 ft) of ground level.*

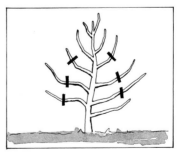

2. *In the second winter, select five or six evenly-spaced lower branches that have a wide angle to the stem. Cut them back to a downward- or outward-facing bud to leave them 25 cm (10 in) long; if they are less than 25 cm (10 in) long, simply remove 2.5 cm (1 in) from the tip.*

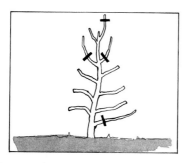

3. At the same time, any other branches at this level should be removed completely. Any branches above this level should be cut back to 15 cm (6 in) to form a second tier. The tip of the main stem is cut back to leave it 30 cm (12 in) above the top branch.

4. Every summer, cut back the tip of each branch to leave 15 cm (6 in) of the current year's growth. Prune side-shoots to 10 cm (4 in) long and any secondary shoots to 5 cm (2 in).

5. Every winter, prune the leading shoot to leave 20 cm (8 in) of the last season's growth.

6. Once the tree has reached the required height and width prune back twice as hard, so that new growth is cut back to 7 cm (3 in) long, side-shoots 5 cm (2 in) long and secondary shoots 2.5 cm (1 in) long.

The simple process of bending branches downwards also has a marked effect on growth. If, for example, you train the branches of climbing roses horizontally, the plant, which still wants to grow upwards to the light, will throw up a number of branches along the top of the tied-down stem. Add to that the fact that the bending restricts the flow of sap, so putting the plant under stress and inducing it to flower, and the advantages of more growth and more flowers are obvious.

The same trick of bending branches is also employed for some fruit trees where the branches are bent quite sharply and tied to the bottom of the trunk. Again, this results in growth on the upper part of the bent branch and more fruit.

Trees, particularly fruit trees, are sometimes manipulated to encourage them to flower or fruit. This is done by disrupting the transport channels which carry sugar and nutrients through the plant. They're situated just below the bark and can be cut by removing a ring of bark. The ring should not, however, run right round the stem or the plant will starve and die, but cutting a band half-way round will put the plant under stress. Its response is to hasten to make seed for the continuation of the line, and, of course, before it can make seed it flowers and fruits.

TRAINING A FESTOONED TREE.

Growth is restricted and trees are encouraged to produce fruiting buds by restricting the flow of sap by bending the branches into severe curves. Great care is needed in bending the branches and it must be done in summer when they are young and supple. Plant trees 1.5 m (5 ft) apart.

1. At the end of the first summer, pull the main shoot downwards, bending it into a hoop. Secure it by tying the end to the base of the tree with soft string.

2. In the second summer, plenty of shoots will grow on top of the curve. Prune these back in summer like cordons (see page 156).

3. Also in the second summer, select more shoots and bend them down into hoops. Secure to the main stem with soft string. Prune any unwanted branches.

4. In subsequent summers prune all the fruiting spurs like cordons. The tree will be permanently bent into a festooned form.

Training a Stepover.

Stepovers are single-tier espaliers, developed to take advantage of every centimetre of space in a small garden. They should be grown on wires strung on short posts 30 cm (12 in) above the ground. Plant trees 3.5–4.5 m (12–15 ft) apart.

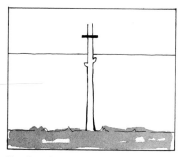

1. Immediately after planting, prune the main stem to 5 cm (2 in) above the wire. Ensure that there are two buds beneath the cut.

2. In the spring, when the buds grow, train the shoots out along the wires, either side of the main stem.

3. Thereafter, each arm is pruned like a cordon (see step 4, page 156). Stop growth when the arms meet those of the next plant.

Fruit growers also make use of their knowledge of apical dominance to shape trees as they want them. One reason the top bud grows fastest is that it sends down a growth-retarding hormone to all the other buds. This is also carried in the cambium layer, just below the bark. If a small nick of bark is removed just above any bud required to grow out, the hormone is diverted and that bud will grow away.

All these practices are quite benign and well within natural 'rules' and so quite acceptable within the Living Garden.

Tree shapes.

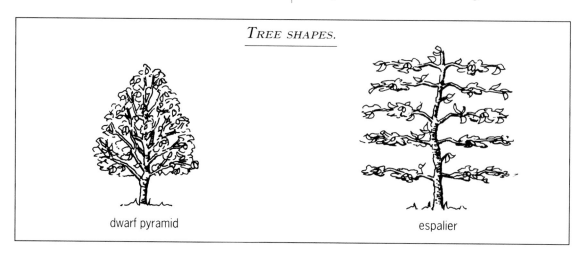

dwarf pyramid

espalier

TREE SHAPES (CONTINUED).

standard tree

bush tree

cordon

festooned tree

fan

stepover

CHAPTER NINE

PROPAGATION – CAPITALISING ON WHAT YOU'VE GOT

Plants have the great disadvantage that they can't move about, so sexual reproduction usually depends on wind or animals transferring pollen from flower to flower. They do successfully set seed but the process is chancy. However, many plants have also evolved means of increasing by vegetative or asexual reproduction, which produces copies of the parent.

We gardeners are very much on nature's side in this respect. We're quite happy to be able to reproduce our favourite plants for free and we can take advantage of their natural methods of doing so.

VEGETATIVE REPRODUCTION

For the plant, the natural advantage of vegetative reproduction is that it can extend the ground it covers, without reproducing sexually. For the gardener, the advantage is that he's guaranteed exact copies in all features of the parent plant.

Often, the parts of the plant used for vegetative reproduction are also storage organs, containing food reserves for the new plant to use as it grows. Potatoes have swollen underground stems, parsnips swollen taproots and onions swollen buds. We sometimes collect and eat the storage organs but the plant's strategy is for them to lie dormant in the soil over winter, and then develop into one or more new plants in the following year. We can exploit that strategy by using them ourselves to produce new plants.

Swollen taproots, such as carrots or parsnips, may not seem at first sight to be a means of producing new plants, but remember that the plants that form them are biennials. After one year, the above-ground parts of the plant wither and die, except for small buds at the base of the stem. In the following year, new shoots develop from these buds, and each is potentially a new plant.

Other plants, like dahlias, store food in swollen roots. In their native countries they survive the winter and develop new plants from buds on the roots in the following

Potatoes are underground stems swollen with food.

Strawberry runners produce new plants at intervals.

year. Dahlias are regularly propagated from these root tubers.

Potatoes are stem tubers. The plant stores food in a swollen underground stem which survives the winter and gives rise to new plants the following year. The 'eyes' on a potato are the buds, each capable of giving rise to a new plant. We usually use small, 'seed' potatoes to start new plants because eating potatoes are sprayed with a chemical used specifically to stop them sprouting. But it is also possible to grow new plants simply by cutting up an ordinary potato and making sure that each piece includes an 'eye' and a portion of the food store. Indeed, you've probably noticed peelings sprouting on the compost heap.

Rhizomes

Some plants, such as bearded irises, produce horizontally-growing underground stems. These are rhizomes and continue to live for many years. Each year, the terminal bud at the end of the underground stem turns up and produces leaves and flowers above

ground, while the lateral bud closest to it continues the growth of the rhizome. Other lateral buds may produce new rhizomes which branch off the parent stem, and these can be carefully broken off and used to start new plants.

Iris, water lilies and Solomon's seal have slow-growing, short and thick rhizomes, which are obviously full of stored food. In others, like mint, Michaelmas daisy and couch-grass, the fast-growing rhizomes are long and thin. We all know how easy it is to start off mint by begging some rhizomes from a neighbour, and how fiendishly-fast couch grass rhizomes invade a garden.

Corms

Corms, formed in plants like crocus and gladiolus, are lumped with bulbs by many gardeners but from the plant's standpoint are rather different. A corm is really a short, swollen, vertically-growing underground stem, forming both a storage organ and a means of propagation. It survives the winter and gives rise to new plants and corms the

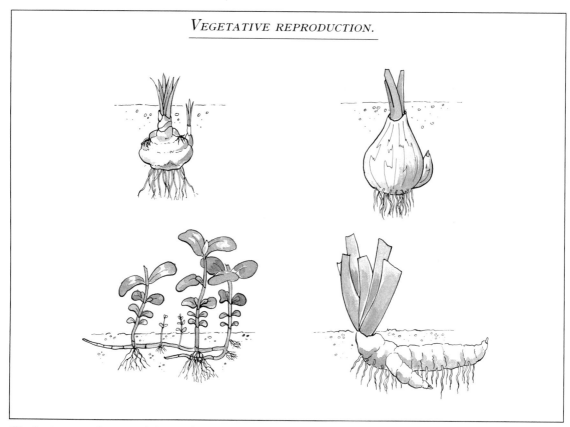

VEGETATIVE REPRODUCTION.

*Clockwise, starting top right, Daffodil bulb with new bulb that has developed from an axillary bud. **Below right**, Rhizome of bearded iris, showing new rhizome developing from lateral bud. **Below left**, Fast-growing mint rhizomes producing new plants from buds. **Top left**, Crocus corm that has produced a new corm on top of the old one, and an additional plant from an axillary bud.*

following year. The terminal bud produces the main plant; axillary buds develop into either additional plants or new corms. New corms form on top of old ones and, as they swell with stored food, they develop special contractile roots that pull them down into the soil and anchor them.

Bulbs

Cut through a bulb, on the other hand, and you'll see that it's really a bud, the leaves having become thick and fleshy with stored food. The base of a bulb is a short stem with roots, and at the centre is the terminal bud which develops into a new plant when winter is over. There are also small axillary buds between the swollen leaf bases and these develop into new bulbs.

We grow many plants from bulbs: daffodils, tulips, snowdrops, hyacinths, bluebells and lilies. Most gardeners leave them in the soil, year in, year out, but if they're lifted, perhaps to make room for other plants, you can easily see the new bulbs that have developed.

Runners

Apart from thin, vigorously-growing rhizomes like those of mint, some plants regularly put out side branches, known as runners or stolons, which develop into new plants. Perhaps the most familiar are strawberry runners, which creep over the ground and form at intervals new strawberry plants, complete with roots. Once the new plants are self-supporting, the intermediate lengths of runner have no function and naturally die off.

We can cut the runners and position the new plants where we want them or we can root them into pots and transplant them somewhere else. Not all runners are long and thin like those of strawberries. Houseleeks (*Sempervivum*), for example, produce short runners called offsets, each of which turns up at the end to form a new plant.

Other plants like brambles and loganberries grow stems so long that their weight causes them to bend over and touch the ground. When they reach the soil, the terminal bud puts out roots and develops into a new plant. If the whole stem reaches the ground it's likely to root at each joint all the way along. New plants can intentionally be produced by pegging the stems to the soil and this is called layering.

It's important to remember that each cell of a plant carries all its genetic information. This means that whole new plants, complete with roots and eventually with flowers, can be produced from leaves or from pieces of stem. So if a plant is damaged it can generally make other plants from the 'bits'.

Mexican hat plants (*Bryophyllum*) have gone so far in this regard that little plants regularly sprout from the notches round the edges of their leaves, even while they're still attached to the parent plant. *Bryophyllum* routinely sheds 'baby' plants and so can spread quickly. Others like *Begonia* and African violets (*Saintpaulia*) can readily be grown from detached leaves or even pieces of leaf.

Most gardeners know that many plants will also produce roots and shoots from pieces of stem, so that if a piece is broken off, perhaps by wind, rain or damage by an animal, it only needs to fall to the ground to root and form a new plant. Indeed the 'Crack Willow' spreads itself along river banks when pieces of branch are broken off in storms and swept downstream. When the branch eventually reaches the bank it roots and forms a new tree.

So-called Egyptian onions (*Allium cepa* 'Viviparum') also demonstrate the fact that all parts of a plant carry all its genetic code or programming. Instead of flowers on the tall 'flowering' stems this onion variety produces clusters of bulbils. These are axillary buds which have become large and fleshy with stored food. In the natural course of events, the bulbils are shed a little distance away from the parent plant, and each develops into a new plant. We can simply detach the bulbils and grow them wherever we wish.

There are many different ways that plants reproduce themselves vegetatively, and the canny gardener can capitalise on this to multiply the number of plants in his garden and greenhouse without buying in new stock.

PLANT PROPAGATION

Over the years, gardeners have devised and perfected several artificial ways of propagating plants. Sometimes these are ways of keeping tender and 'difficult' plants going and very often they're the one way of producing plants that are identical in every respect. Since production from seed always results in variations, vegetative propagation is particularly valuable for multiplying hybrids, whose special features would be lost in sexual reproduction and seed formation.

Artificial propagation depends on the fact that some parts of plants, like the shoot tips and areas near the surface of shoots and roots, retain the ability to grow. Under special circumstances these areas can be induced to form different sorts of plant tissue, such as new stems and roots.

Layering

The method of propagation closest to plants' natural habit is layering. It involves putting part of a stem in the ground and leaving it attached to the parent until it has developed roots.

So-called tip layering is used mainly for plants like blackberries and loganberries which naturally reproduce vegetatively when their long shoots come into contact with the soil. In late summer, pull down as many shoots as you need and make a hole in the soil where the tip of each shoot rests. Place the tip in the hole and pin it in position using a forked stick. Cover the tip with soil and leave it until the leaves of the parent plant fall. You can then cut the 'layer' from the parent, lift it, and transplant the new plant to its permanent position.

Normal layering involves burying a length of the shoot with the tip exposed, and leaving it to root. It's usually done in early spring for shrubs and in early summer for climbers, and is suitable for plants that root less readily than the briar fruits, like *Rhododendron, Clematis, Abelia*, some *Viburnum, Magnolia, Hamamelis, Choisya, Camellia* and *Azalea*.

Egyptian onions produce clusters of bulbils instead of flowers. These drop off and form new plants.

LAYERING.

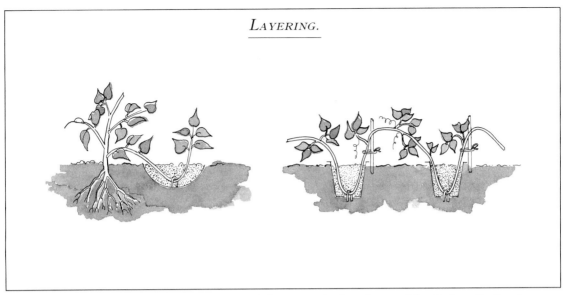

Plant propagation by **(left)** *normal layering and* **(right)** *serpentine layering, used for climbers. Rooting is encouraged by sharply twisting or nicking the underside of the stems before burying them.*

Mexican hat plants Bryophyllum *sprout little plants from notches around their leaves.*

Rooting can be encouraged by twisting the stem firmly to rupture the tissues before burying it or by cutting a slit on the underside. You can tell when the 'layer' has rooted by its fresher and more vigorous appearance. It can often be removed from the parent plant in the following autumn but in some plants rooting takes much longer. Rhododendrons, for instance, take two or even three years.

Clematis and other climbers can be induced to produce several plants from one stem by what is known as serpentine layering. Wound the stem by slitting it at intervals along its length near to a bud and bury each damaged section. When shoots start growing from each 'layer', they can be separated from each other and from the parent plant, and replanted.

Division

Herbaceous perennials can be propagated by division of the root clump and, indeed, most perennials benefit from division. The old centre of the plant becomes less vigorous with age and is best discarded. In autumn or spring, lift the whole root clump with a fork. If it has all been growing and flowering healthily, simply divide it into two, either by pulling it apart with the hands or a trowel or, if the root system is very matted, lever it apart with two forks placed back to back. If, however, the centre of the clump is old and useless, break new shoots and roots from the edge of the clump and replant them.

Plants with fleshy roots, like plantain lilies (*Hosta*), are best lifted in spring, when you can see new buds and so know where to cut. Divide the roots with a spade or sharp knife, making sure that each piece has at least one good bud, and replant immediately.

DIVIDING PERENNIALS

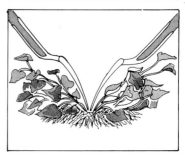

1. Lift the entire plant out of the border and divide it in half. If it has a large, matted root system, stick two garden forks back to back into the centre of the clump and force it apart.

2. Remove the young shoots from the outer side of the clump by breaking or cutting them off.

3. Cut all the leaves right back to within 2.5 cm (1 in) of the roots and replant immediately or pot up in potting compost and put the pots in a shady area until you can replant them.

Cuttings

Taking cuttings is perhaps the commonest method of propagation. Tender perennials root very easily from side shoots. Take cuttings of dahlias, cosmos and some salvias in spring, and cuttings of fuchsias, geraniums (*Pelargonium*) and chrysanthemums in late summer or early autumn.

Remove a healthy side shoot just above a leaf joint, making the cutting about 7.5 cm (3 in) long. Trim with a really sharp knife, cutting just below the bottom leaf joint, and remove the bottom leaves. The small leafy stipules under the leaf stems of geraniums should also be removed. You need to leave about four leaves if they're small, as in fuchsias, but can get away with two if they're large, as in geraniums.

Cuttings from most plants will benefit from dipping the cut end into a hormone rooting powder. They can then be dibbled 5 cm (2 in) apart into a compost consisting of equal parts of coir and horticultural vermiculite. Set the pot or tray of cuttings inside a propagator to give gentle bottom heat of about 20°C (68°F), and they should root in a couple of weeks. Geraniums don't like too humid an atmosphere so these will be better on an open bench in the greenhouse. Once the cuttings have rooted and look healthy, transfer them to 7.5 cm (3 in) pots of soilless potting compost.

Softwood cuttings can be taken from many shrubs in June. Cut strong, young shoots in their first year of growth, cutting just above a leaf joint so that they're 7.5–10 cm (3–4 in) long. If you're away from home, keep them fresh in a polythene bag until you get back and can deal with them.

TAKING SOFTWOOD CUTTINGS

1. Take cuttings of healthy, young plant shoots about 10 cm (4 in) long. Cut back by half just below a leaf joint.

2. Carefully trim away all the side leaves then dip the cutting in fungicide solution.

3. Dip the end of the cutting into hormone rooting powder and shake off the excess. Then plant in a seed tray containing equal parts of peat and perlite. Space in rows 2.5 cm (1 in) apart each way.

4. Water using a fungicide solution. Wrap the tray in light polythene sheeting so that the sheeting touches the tops of the cuttings and is sealed under the tray. Put the tray into a cold frame.

Prepare them by trimming just below a leaf joint and remove the lower leaves as for tender perennials. Dip them in hormone rooting powder and put them into a pot or tray filled with equal parts of coir and horticultural vermiculite. Cover them with very thin, clear polythene (the thickness dry-cleaners use for covering clothes is ideal), tucking it underneath so that it's airtight, making sure that the polythene actually touches the cuttings. Put them in a cold frame, shaded with a layer of onion net or plastic greenhouse netting. The idea is to strike a balance between giving the cuttings sufficient light for photosynthesis but not so much sunlight that they wilt. In very bright or dull weather, more or less shade may be desirable and you will have to judge whether to add a second layer of netting or remove it altogether. In six to eight weeks the cuttings should have rooted and can then be individually potted. Conifer cuttings root better if the bottom of the shoot is bruised, so pull the leaves off rather than cutting them.

Many shrubs, like willows, flowering currant, forsythia, buddleia, dogwood and mock orange, root readily from hardwood cuttings, and nothing could be easier. Simply cut 23 cm (9 in) lengths of shoot from the current season's wood in autumn. Trim the top end to just above a leaf joint and the bottom to just below a joint and plant the cuttings firmly in garden soil so that about 7.5 cm (3 in) shows above the soil. Rooting is helped, especially in heavy soil, if you put a layer of sharp sand in the bottom of the cuttings trench. In the following autumn, when each cutting has a good root system, transplant them 15–23 cm (6–9 in) apart in rows. After a second year, they'll be ready to be moved to their permanent positions.

A few plants, like sea kale, horseradish,

TAKING HARDWOOD CUTTINGS.

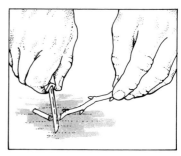

1. Cut off a length of stem about 20–23 cm (8–9 in) long, using a sharp knife. Trim it below the lowest bud and cut off the soft top growth by trimming just above a bud.

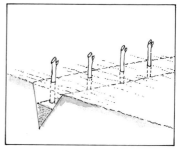

2. Make a narrow trench and line the bottom with sharp sand. Place the cuttings in the trench, leaving 7.5 cm (3 in) of the top out of the ground. Refill the trench, firm in the cuttings and leave them for one year.

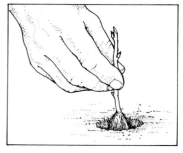

3. The following winter, plant them approximately 15–23 cm (6–9 in) apart in rows in a corner of the garden. Leave them for another year, then transplant them to their permanent position in the garden.

delphiniums and Japanese anemones, are propagated by root cuttings taken during the winter. Sections of thick root about 10 cm (4 in) long are cut and trimmed so that the upper end is square but the lower slanted. This is purely so that you know which end is which and don't put them in upside down. Put them in coir compost so that the top is just below the surface of the soil, and put the pots in a cold frame. In spring the top end will develop shoots and when they're big enough they can be planted out.

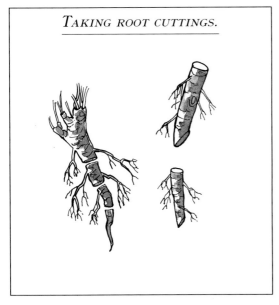

TAKING ROOT CUTTINGS.

Taking root cuttings from plants such as horseradish. Trimming the lower end to a slant will ensure that you plant them the correct way up.

African violets, tuberous begonias and gloxinias can be grown from leaf cuttings in the greenhouse. With begonias and gloxinias, the leaves are pinned down on to the surface of the compost, making sure they lay quite flat. The pot or tray is then best placed in a propagator as it needs gentle warmth (about 20°C or 68°F) and constant humidity, although it mustn't be allowed to get wet. With African violets, cut off a youngish leaf including a piece of the leaf stalk. Stick these into compost, leaf stalk down, generally putting two, back to back, in each pot. Again, put the pots in a propagator and they should all root in about three to four weeks.

Cape primroses Streptocarpus, *like African violets, tuberous begonias and gloxinias, can be propagated from leaf cuttings.*

Grafting and budding

If, in nature, two tree branches constantly rub together they sometimes eventually join naturally. Gardeners use extremely sophisticated methods to achieve the same result by grafting and budding. The methods are generally used to put a variety of perhaps a rose, a fruit tree or an ornamental shrub on to a special rootstock. This is done for a variety of reasons: the rootstock may be more or less vigorous than the variety's own roots, or it may be resistant to pests or diseases. Sometimes grafting is used to put a second variety on to a fruit tree to provide a pollinator (see page 124).

CLEFT GRAFTING.

Cleft grafting is used to graft a new variety on to an existing tree.

1. In mid-winter, prepare the limb where you will site the graft by cutting back two branches just above a fork.

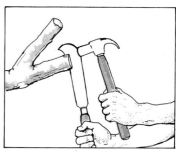

2. Towards the end of winter or in early spring, just as the tree is starting its new growth, split each of the cut ends by driving a billhook into each one with a hammer.

3. Prepare four lengths of stem (known as scion) from the required variety. Each scion should be of one-year-old growth and about 10–15 cm (4–6 in) long. Cut the base of each one to form a wedge shape.

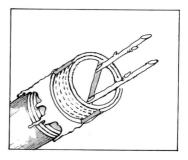

4. Insert scions into each cut end, making sure the cambium layers (the layers just below the bark) correspond. Tie in the scions using raffia or string and cover the wounds with grafting wax.

WHIP-AND-TONGUE GRAFTING.

Whip-and-tongue grafting is used to graft a variety on to a rootstock.

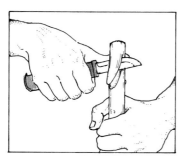

1. Trim the rootstock right back and, with a sharp knife, make a long, slanting cut in the top part of the stem to leave a long wedge shape.

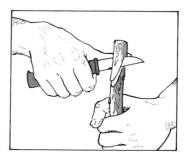

2. Using a one-year-old scion, cut the end to form a corresponding wedge.

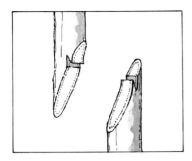

3. Make two more cuts, one upwards in the rootstock and one downwards in the scion, to form two 'tongues' that will fit together.

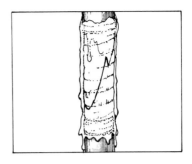

4. Fit the scion into the rootstock, making sure that the cambium layers correspond. Tie the graft with raffia and cover the wound with grafting wax.

Basically, a shoot of the variety (the scion), is inserted into a slit in the bark of a rooted plant (the stock). The essentials to note are that the cuts need to be smooth so that there's intimate contact between the scion and the stock and that the two cambium layers just below the bark are in contact. That's where the joining potential is located.

In budding, the scion consists only of a bud, sometimes with a small portion of the outer part of the stem on which it originally grew. Not only must there be intimate contact between the tissues of the scion and the stock so the two are bound tightly together but usually the entire junction is also covered with grafting wax to stop it drying out. Not surprisingly, grafting of different species rarely works.

Vegetative propagation versus *seed production*

When a plant multiplies vegetatively in nature or when gardeners propagate existing stock, the consequences for both plant and gardener are very different from those of seed production.

When plants are vegetatively produced, whether naturally, like bulb production, or artificially, like taking cuttings, the new plants carry exactly the same genetic information as the parent so they're always accurate copies.

But when a plant flowers, is pollinated and sets seed it's quite a different story. The genes of both parents are carried in their offspring but the results you see can be very different. For example, the plant may carry the genes for both tall and short but if tall is dominant the plant will be tall. However, that short gene is still there so some plants in the next generation could be short. Sexual reproduction, in other words, is a lottery in terms of end-product.

For plant and gardener, this lottery gives the possibility of the production of new varieties which may be more colourful, hardier or more vigorous than the parent. Just as likely, however, is that some will be duller, less hardy or weaker. Vegetative reproduction, on the other hand, is a guaranteed method of producing copies. For a plant 'interested' in spreading, and for the gardener anxious to capitalise on what he has, it's foolproof.

It's nevertheless important to stress that we gardeners often have much to gain from harvesting seeds as a source of new plants. Many commonly grown garden annuals, perennials, shrubs and trees will breed true and some with enough slight variation to make it a fascinating and exciting project.

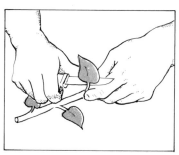

*1. In summer, cut a length of stem from the variety
you want to bud. Leaving the leaf stalks on the cutting,
remove all the leaves. (If you are budding a rose,
remove the thorns first.) Immerse the whole stem in a
bowl of water until it is needed.*

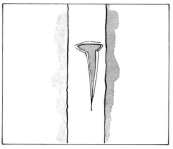

*2. With a sharp knife, cut a T-shaped slit in the bark
at the rootstock and peel back the bark very slightly.*

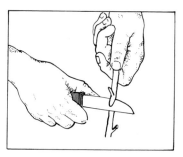

*3. Remove a bud from the prepared stem – insert a
sharp knife below the bud and pull it upwards,
keeping the knife just under the bud.*

*4. Examine the base of the bud carefully and you will
see a sliver of wood in the centre. Remove it with your
fingernail.*

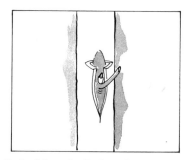

*5. Slide the bud into the T-shaped slit using the leaf
stalk as a handle. When he bud is secure, cut away
any excess bark to ensure a perfect fit and tie the bud
on to the tree using raffia or a special rubber tie.*

Lawns are encouraged by regular mowing to produce a dense, resilient turf.

LAWNS

Leave a lawn unmown in summer, even for only a couple of weeks, and the grass grows so much that it soon ceases to look like a lawn. Leave it for a whole season and the grasses flower, other plants grow tall and it becomes a meadow. Attractive it may be, but to serve its function the grass has to be kept short, forming a dense, resilient turf.

Lawn grasses have a method of growth and a way of vegetative reproduction that make them particularly suitable for the job. We encourage that natural habit by regular mowing: one way in which we gardeners constantly manipulate nature.

Most good lawn grasses are tufted perennials which spread by means of underground stems (rhizomes) that produce an abundance of leafy shoots. The buds that thicken the tuft and produce the spreading rhizomes are developed at or below ground level, where they're protected from trampling and the action of the lawn-mower by the bases of old leaf shoots and by the soil. Cutting the leaves prevents the production of flowering stems and stimulates the development of buds into shoots.

The growth zone of a grass leaf is right at the base, so the tip is the oldest part. New growth from the base pushes up the entire blade, until the leaf is fully expanded, so that after the tip is removed it appears to be replaced. If you cut the worn end from a daisy or rose leaf, there is no growth replacement because their mode of development is quite different. As you mow away worn ends of grass leaves, however, growth from below makes good what you've removed. Repeated mowing consequently improves grass quality, as well as promoting the establishment of thick, dense turf.

Of course, grasses evolved this growth form long before there were lawn mowers to encourage it. But there were natural 'lawn-mowers', namely grazing animals like antelope, cattle, deer and horses. The peculiarities of grass developed way back in time as a response to the grass-cropping habits of those grazing animals. We are now reaping the benefits of this close association of grasses and grazers.

Regular cutting of grass not only improves its quality but also discourages other sorts of plants because they keep getting their heads chopped off. Some plants, however, can happily co-exist with lawn-mowers because of low, compact growth and short flowering stems. Lawn purists take steps to remove these 'weeds' and feel that to do otherwise would be nothing short of heresy but their different leaf shapes and colours add variety to turf.

The moss-like leaves of buttonweed, the feathery fronds of yarrow, the yellow and red flowers of bird's-foot-trefoil, the downy leaves and brown flowers of field wood-rush, the purple flowers of self-heal, the tight, creamy flowerheads of clover and the white 'stars' of daisies all make the average lawn a garden in miniature. Dandelions and plantains are best dug out with a knife because their spreading leaves smother the grass but the others can add to the enjoyment of a lawn. They spring back after trampling and in no way detract from compact cover of the ground.

For most people, the lawn is an important part of their garden, so much so, that a study in California produced some rather startling statistics. Keeping a lawn 'reasonably attractive' in California's hot climate took a greater input of energy (in terms of labour, power for irrigation, energy content of fertilisers, and so on) per square metre than is needed to grow maize, an important food crop.

CHAPTER TEN

THE COMPLETE GARDEN

It should be obvious that the function of a garden, as far as we're concerned, is to grow plants. You no doubt enjoy working hard to create beautiful borders and a productive fruit and vegetable plot and, like all gardeners, you get a great kick out of seeing strong, healthy growth.

But when you make and maintain a garden you, perhaps unwittingly, also have an enormous influence on a world of other living creatures who make their home in your patch. Some, as far as the gardener's concerned, are pests, some are predators and others are neither. Together, they form an interdependent chain of life that's mutually beneficial.

What we must all understand is that, far from being casual observers, we're actually part of that huge and complex chain which starts with the tiniest microbe in the soil and finishes with us. But, make no mistake, that microbe is just as important to the chain of life as we are and without it our lives would certainly be poorer. It's not just that the microbe makes plant food available

and therefore encourages better plant growth but that possibly another organism lives on it, something else eats that and so on right up the chain.

On the other hand, we can't just let our gardens be taken over by nature or we'd finish up with a wilderness. So we must act as umpires, gently influencing events, doing no more than directing natural forces in the way we want them to go. We do after all have an evolutionary advantage but we must make sure that we use it wisely to protect all the lower forms of life upon whom we surely depend.

If you do that, you'll finish up with a garden that's busily buzzing with all kinds of wild creatures, some seen and some not so obvious. And you'll create for yourself another fascinating, absorbing and beautiful dimension to your gardening.

THE ECOLOGY OF THE GARDEN

One of the things we gardeners soon come to accept is that many more plants and

*A rich, well-structured garden (**left***) is home to an astonishing variety of animals. Some are pests, but many are predators controlling the plant-eaters.* **Above***, plants like this dandelion, and animals too, produce many more offspring than can survive.*

animals are produced than survive. Death in the garden, as anywhere, is commonplace and some of it's intentional. If you successfully grew and maintained *all* the plants that are produced from every packet of seeds, you'd simply have to go into the nursery business. Most have to be discarded, and only the healthiest seedlings are grown on.

And that's exactly what happens naturally. Look at how many seeds are carried by dandelions in their powder-puff 'clocks', yet we aren't overrun by dandelions. The blue-tits using a nest box in the garden lay up to a dozen eggs but, before they grow into adult birds, most disappear, many nestlings dying in the nest. The enormous potential for increase in numbers that plants and animals have is never realised because of high mortality. There are so many young plants and animals jostling for space, nutrients or food that there's fierce competition. It's rarely evident as out-and-out conflict, but it's none the less very real.

The garden's inhabitants compete for what they need, both with other members of the same species and with other species. A row of seedling lettuces, for example, has to be drastically thinned or they'll all suffer. Gardeners remedy this by ensuring that all plants have sufficient space to satisfy their demands and to grow healthy and strong.

Competition between plants of different species is again eased, if not entirely eliminated, by ensuring that each plant has sufficient room for its growth and development. If you don't do this, the results will be all too obvious. Plants too close to a hedge, for example, won't grow properly and all plants, including grass growing within the zone of a birch tree's thirsty roots will suffer. Remember though, that if you've created a deep and fertile soil you can get away with much closer planting than is usually recommended.

Animals in the garden are also in competition with each other for food and living space. Gardeners entice in so-called pests by satisfying their demands, particularly for food, by growing tender and appetising vegetables. But you can reduce their depredations by cultural methods, like hoeing round plants, by mixed planting, and by encouraging natural predators.

Above all, we must never forget that the garden maintains a complex, interconnecting web of feeding activities. Plants are eaten by herbivorous animals, including pests such as aphids, but they in turn are eaten by carnivores, such as predatory hoverfly larvae. Hoverflies are eaten by spiders, wasps and birds, and there's a vast network of consumption, predators eating other predators as well as herbivores.

Everything that dies, whether it be plant or animal, is eaten and ultimately decomposed by bacteria and fungi. We depend on the functioning of the food-web for consumption of pests by predators, for the breakdown and disappearance of all dead animals and plants, and for the recycling of the nitrogen compounds and other nutrients that they contain. A healthy garden is one where all these natural events are proceeding uninterrupted, and you interfere with them at your peril.

If, for example, you cart away all dead material to the tip, you remove the plant base on which the decomposer food-chain rests, and there will be few nutrients to be released back into the soil. This will then deteriorate and become less able to support and nurture the garden's plants.

If you spray chemical insecticides on caterpillars there's a serious risk that blue-tits or blackbirds will take on a magnified dose of the poisons by eating dying caterpillars. You may end up poisoning these useful allies and you may even kill a sparrowhawk that preys on them. Worse still, without the natural controllers, you may be driven to use more and more insecticide, poisoning the environment and ultimately, as animals die, the soil. As so many 'reliable' insecticides are non-biodegradable, you may even end up killing earthworms and other animals on which soil health depends, eventually affecting the nourishment and growth of your plants. This may seem like an extremely pessimistic outlook but so interdependent are the elements of the garden food-web, that it's a real possibility and not worth the risk.

The amount and variety of animal life in a garden, or anywhere else, is dependent on the quantity and diversity of plants. Animals depend ultimately on plants harnessing the sun's energy and turning it into chemical energy. It's transferred from plants to the herbivores (which we call 'pests'), and then to predators to power all their life processes. But that means, of course, that there must be an upper limit. You can't have predators without the plant-feeders and the number of those depends on the amount of plant material they have to feed on. Bear in mind too, that there will always be more herbivores than carnivores. But most predators are not too fussy about their choice of food, particularly the higher-level ones towards the top of the food-chain. So it follows that the more diverse your garden plants, the more effective the predators will be. The message is to plant as big an assortment of different plants as possible.

Gardening also depends on the fact that materials are reused again and again in a vast recycling operation. The wise and thrifty gardener makes the most of this by ensuring that all dead or unwanted plant material goes on to the compost heap, where animals and bacteria break it down into a form that can once again be taken up by plants. Working compost into the soil boosts nutrient levels and also improves soil condition so that plant roots grow healthily and strongly. By exploiting natural recycling, gardeners can ensure that plants are provided with perfect growing conditions. Never forget that plants, animals and the non-living environment, like soil and water, form a complex, largely self-supporting system powered by the absorption of light energy by plants. The more subsidies we put into the system in the form of work (energy) and materials (like manure and fertilisers), the more dividends we can take out as produce. Work hard in your garden, improving the soil and cultivating the plants, and you'll reap ample rewards.

GEOFF HAMILTON'S BARNSDALE GARDEN

Almost all accounts of garden wildlife are anecdotal and vague. There's a general feeling that encouraging predators is a good thing, and that variety in the garden provides the ideal situation, but there's very little hard evidence of what's actually there and what the animals are doing.

The $5\frac{1}{2}$-acre garden at Barnsdale has never been sprayed with any pesticide and only organic fertilisers have ever been used. While there has never been a serious attempt to assess the effect of this policy on wildlife, the results are fairly obvious. After all, it has to be good enough for up to six million gardeners to see every week!

It's interesting to compare the soil of this garden with that of the chemically-farmed field next door. The mineral content is the same but the soil in the field is hard and lumpy, difficult to break down, always compacted and waterlogged in winter, whereas the Barnsdale soil is fine, crumbly and black with organic matter. What's more, every spadeful brings up half-a-dozen worms while you could dig all day next door and never find one. The Barnsdale soil is the result of digging in and mulching over 100 tonnes of farmyard manure every year while the farmland's state can be put down to nothing but chemical fertilisers.

At Barnsdale there's a multitude of insects, hedgehogs, frogs, toads by the hundreds and occasional visits from foxes, deer and badgers. These last are less welcome but are fascinating to watch and cause little damage. When the wildlife pool was first installed it took precisely a week for the first shimmering dragonfly to make itself at home.

Many visitors have remarked particularly on the abundance of birdsong. BBC sound

recordists have ears professionally tuned for extraneous noises so it's especially pleasing when they remark on the deafening din of the Barnsdale birds. All the common ones are there, plus regular visits from barn owls, tawny owls and even, just now and then, an amazing nightingale.

There's no doubt that all this wildlife adds another fascinating interest to gardening as well as keeping down the pests. Without spraying, there are virtually no pest problems except the slugs in the hostas. And even the most ardent of pellet-pushers have those.

But without the time, the facilities or the expertise to quantify the amount of wildlife that has been attracted to Barnsdale, all this is somewhat anecdotal too. Jenny Owen, on the other hand, is probably the only entomologist and ecologist in this country who can give definite answers.

Jennifer Owen's suburban garden

Jenny has been investigating the wildlife of her garden, as well as actively gardening, for twenty years. It's not a large garden, less than $\frac{1}{5}$ acre, and it's not only definitely suburban but on the corner of a main road. The lawn's well-trimmed, the paths neat, and the garden's productive in terms of flowers for the house, produce for the kitchen, and even logs for the fire. But the vegetation is more varied and lush than is the norm in suburban gardens. It wouldn't win a conventional best-kept garden competition but it's nevertheless a beautiful and interesting place.

At one time or another since 1972, nearly 300 species of flowering plant have been cultivated in the garden, and almost 100

Wildlife pool and bog garden on Geoff Hamilton's varied $5\frac{1}{2}$ acres at Barnsdale.

additional species, many of them so-called weeds, have come in of their own accord. In addition, 24 species of grass have been present, either as lawn grasses or as weeds, nine different sorts of moss have been found, and 25 sorts of toadstools have appeared, many of them when, out of interest, the lawn was left unmown one autumn. The diversity of plants provides a firm base on which a great variety of interconnecting food-chains have developed.

Twenty-two species of butterflies have been recorded in the garden, some often, others less so, three of them only once. Five species, small and large whites (the cabbage whites), the green-veined white, the brimstone and the orange-tip, breed in the garden on a variety of (mainly cruciferous) plants; all the others are visitors for flower nectar.

Three hundred and forty-three different sorts of moths have been identified, of which 68 have bred in the garden, the caterpillars using a total of 115 different species of plants. Like the butterflies, most moths visit to feed on nectar at the many garden flowers.

Bees make good use of the garden's nectar and pollen resources, there being, apart from the honey-bee, 13 sorts of bumble-bees and 37 species of solitary bees. It's not known how many actually breed in the garden but some certainly do.

Of the other groups of animals which are mainly plant-feeders, there are 58 sorts of sawflies, of which ten breed in the garden, at least 42 different species of plant-sucking bugs (including aphids), several species of flies whose larvae eat plant material, many sorts of plant-eating beetles, and 17 sorts of

The animals of Jenny Owen's suburban garden have been intensively investigated for twenty years.

slugs and snails. This may sound an alarming catalogue of plant-eaters but there are never any real pest problems because there is also an impressive list of predators.

Of the 91 species of hoverflies recorded, some commonly, others rarely, 57 have predatory larvae that feed on aphids, and nine of these definitely breed in the garden. Six species of social wasps have been identified, 34 of solitary wasps, and 557 (yes, that's not a mis-print, 557) of parasitic wasps.

There are at least 64 sorts of spiders, ten of harvestmen, 26 species of ground beetles, 11 species of ladybirds, 18 of lacewings and their relatives, and 52 sorts of predatory bugs, as well as such ubiquitous predators as ants. The tally of beetles is over 250 species, of which many in addition to ground beetles and ladybirds are predatory.

The total list of insects in the garden, so far, is well over 1,600 species, and there are more than 120 sorts of other invertebrate animals, including centipedes, spiders and harvestmen. The soil fauna, apart from earthworms, has not been investigated but must include hundreds of sorts of nematodes, mites, collembolans and microscopic organisms.

Then there are the vertebrate animals, including three sorts of amphibians, 49 of birds and seven of mammals. The bird list includes many only seen flying over the garden but 15 species have nested there at least once, and the majority of these are insect-eaters. It's no wonder that there are no pest problems in a garden so well supplied with predators.

The majority of the garden list of more than 1,780 recorded species of animals are undoubtedly feeding there, even though by no means all breed there, and about 50 per cent of these are carnivores. The plant-eaters may all be common but they have to cope

with an impressive array of predators. The point to emphasise is that this is not just a wildlife garden but also a gardener's garden. Animal life is tolerated and encouraged but the plants are nurtured and prized.

CREATING THE COMPLETE GARDEN

The first and most important thing to get right is the soil. Dig deep, at least initially, incorporating plenty of compost or manure, and thereafter keep the soil in good heart with lots of organic material and good drainage. Correct any acidity with lime applications, and work the soil well before sowing seeds or putting in plants.

It's well worth planting to a plan rather than haphazardly so, before even sowing seeds, think what the overall design is to be. Of course, this will depend on the size of plot you have available, the aspect, and the direction of the prevailing wind but ideally you should aim for a rich diversity of plants and of structure.

The variety of a rich garden, with unexpected corners and plantings, different views wherever you go and, ideally, different levels, is far easier on the eye and much more interesting than regimented blocks of plants and geometrically straight paths. Great mounds of vegetation are always more attractive than a few stark silhouettes.

What's more, a garden with many different sorts of plants in a mosaic of open places and shady nooks will be home to a wide variety of different animals.

Even on a small plot, aim to have at least one tree, and consider a hedge or a row of cordoned fruit trees as an alternative to fences and walls. If you're stuck with a wall

Poppies, hostas and other plants give good ground cover and lots of shelter for animals in this garden.

A row of cordon-trained fruit trees, such as these pears, forms a hedge and makes an attractive and productive alternative to a fence or wall.

or a not particularly attractive fence, grow climbers up it, or an espalier tree. Aim to put every square inch of your land to attractive and productive use. If the soil is rich and well-maintained it should have no difficulty in supporting this intensive use.

Once you have plants growing in the garden, you'll need to cater for their needs in terms of water, light and nutrients. In a natural garden there should be few problems with pests and a large measure of control of any you do have will come from natural predators. Aim for total ground cover, even by non-invasive and low-

Espalier-trained apples not only hide unsightly walls and fences but also provide sheltered nesting sites for blackbirds, robins, wrens and other birds.

growing weeds. This, along with mixed planting and good structural diversity, should encourage a natural balance of plant-eaters and predators in the garden.

No garden, however small, should be without a pond. Any frogs, toads and newts that use it will also spend a lot of time out of the water, eating garden insects. Furthermore, frogs and other amphibians have declined sadly in numbers with the disappearance and pollution of field ponds, so you'll also be doing your bit for conservation. A pond can be as small as a sunken washing-up bowl or as large and

Fan-training is usually used for peaches or nectarines but this pear is effectively covering a wall whose reflected and stored heat will ripen the fruit early.

landscaped as a mini-lake but it adds enormously to the attractiveness and interest of a garden.

As well as providing a home for amphibians, birds visit ponds to drink, and a variety of insects, some colourful and dashing like dragonflies, are attracted to the water. Pond plants will bring with them the snails, tiny crustaceans and other animals that make pond-water teem with life.

If frogs, toads or newts use the pond, make sure there's a shelving bank or some arrangement of stones or logs so that the tiny froglets, toadlets and newts can get out of the water on to dry land. Just one word of warning: if you have small children it's perhaps best to wait until they're older before making a pond.

An abundance of bird life is definitely a good thing in a garden, not least because of all the caterpillars, aphids and other insects they eat and feed to their young. Dense vegetation (particularly shrubbery), climbers against walls or fences, and tall or spreading trees will encourage birds of many sorts to nest. Nests in such places will be safe, and you can make good a lack of tree-holes by putting up a couple of nest boxes for hole-nesting species. If you're lucky enough to find birds' nests, don't disturb them when the adults are sitting on eggs or feeding nestlings, or you may cause them to desert. So dissuade your children from checking regularly on the eggs and babies.

Many birds that spend a lot of time in gardens, like blackbirds and starlings, regularly eat berries. Robins, song thrushes and warblers do so occasionally too. Good berry crops will bring mistle thrushes to gardens, and also some of the winter visitors to England such as redwings and fieldfares. If you're really lucky when colourful waxwings arrive in England, a show of bright berries are likely to entice some to visit and feed in your garden. So when you're planning your planting, include some fruit-bearing plants for the birds. They like holly, *Pyracantha*, *Cotoneaster*, hawthorn, wild-type roses, crab-apples, rowan, guelder-rose, honeysuckle, white beam, elder and many more.

In the winter, particularly when the ground's frozen, feeding is difficult for many common garden birds, and they'll appreciate a bird table stocked with peanuts, wild birdseed, sunflower seeds, special bird cake, suet and kitchen scraps – and, of course, a container of water. It'll keep them alive through the winter. But don't leave the bird table out once the nesting season starts because parent birds will find it much easier to stock up there rather than catching the insects and spiders their nestlings need. And, surprisingly, they'll almost certainly choke the hungry baby bird with indigestible bread and peanuts.

If you have a cat, there's little you can do to entice birds into a small garden. Indeed you probably shouldn't try, for you might only be luring them to their deaths.

Flower-feeding insects are interesting and beautiful, and most are pollinators. Many also have predatory larvae (like the majority of common hoverflies) or themselves catch plant-feeding insects for their young (like wasps).

The classic 'butterfly flowers' are those with deep, slender flower tubes, like valerian, *Phlox*, *Dianthus*, thistles and cornflowers, but butterflies also feed successfully at shallower flowers, like *Rudbeckia*, African and French marigolds (*Tagetes erecta* and *Tagetes patula*). And, of course, no gardener who likes to see butterflies should be without a butterfly bush (*Buddleia davidii*), whose fruity scent and copious nectar act like a magnet. The common variety with long, pale mauve

Garden pools attract birds to drink and bathe, amphibians to breed, and dragonflies to lay eggs.

Pyracantha *berries attract birds such as visiting*
redwings, fieldfares and waxwings in winter.

The flowers of Convolvulus minor *with their bright*
yellow centres are especially attractive to feeding
hoverflies.

Densely-planted corners like this collection of rhododendron, hostas, Pennisetum *grass, fuchsia, and* Enkianthus
shelter nesting birds, small mammals, spiders and many insects.

A bird-table well-stocked with peanuts, coconut, fat and grain is especially valuable in winter.

plants flower. You should aim to have flowers in your garden in all months of the year and certainly, as far as insects are concerned, from April to October. Butterflies and hoverflies are so abundant in gardens in late summer and early autumn because they find many more flowers at which they can feed in gardens than they do in hedgerows, meadows and woodland glades. This is because we grow so many North American plants like Michaelmas daisies and goldenrod, along with plants like the iceplant from China, that flower later here in our cooler summers.

There are some cultural practices which orthodox gardeners might baulk at that provide valuable insect food in the form of flowers. Butterflies love the curious-smelling flowers of privet so if you can leave a section of hedge untrimmed long enough for it to flower, they'll visit to feed. They're also very partial to the flowers of many of the cruciferous plants we cultivate as vegetables. So leave a plant or two of cabbage, broccoli or radish to flower, and butterflies will enjoy them.

THE COMPLETE GARDEN

The secret of the complete garden is that it's a microcosm of the natural world, where the growth of plants, the activities of micro-organisms in the soil, and the busy lives of the animals that populate the garden are allowed to proceed without interference. True, the gardener influences the outcome of many of the natural events but he doesn't dominate or attempt to fit the garden into a straitjacket. Rather, wise gardeners use their knowledge and understanding to manipulate gently the plants and animals.

They don't dowse a structureless soil with inorganic chemical fertilisers to promote plant growth but instead use bulky organic

flowerheads is best.

The more bright, colourful, scented flowers there are in a garden, the better it will attract flower-feeding insects by its gaudy advertisement of nectar and pollen. All gardeners have their favourite flowers and specialities but there is a wealth of possibilities to choose from. On the opposite page are some ideas.

One thing to remember, particularly when choosing varieties, is that by and large insects have difficulty feeding at double flowers with great froths of petals. So, if you're interested in insect visitors, choose the single varieties of such flowers as asters and French marigolds.

Another point to watch is the time that

Flowers attractive to insects

Insect flowers	Principal visitors
Hollyhock *Althaea rosea*	Bees
Snapdragon *Antirrhinum majus*	Bees
Columbine *Aquilegia hybrida*	Butterflies, bees
Michaelmas daisy *Aster novi-belgii*	Butterflies, bees, hoverflies
Borage *Borago officinalis*	Bees
Butterfly bush *Buddleia davidii*	Butterflies, bees
Pot marigold *Calendula officinalis*	Hoverflies
Aster *Callistephus chinensis*	Hoverflies
Cornflowers *Centaurea cyanus*	Butterflies
Perennial cornflower *Centaurea montana*	Butterflies
Valerian *Centranthus ruber*	Butterflies, moths
Marguerite *Chrysanthemum frutescens*	Hoverflies
Dwarf convolvulus *Convolvulus minor*	Hoverflies
Sweet Williams *Dianthus barbatus*	Butterflies, moths
Foxglove *Digitalis purpurea*	Bees
Globe thistle *Echinops ritro*	Butterflies, bees
Viper's bugloss *Echium plantagineum*	Bees
Fennel *Foeniculum vulgare*	Hoverflies
Dame's-violet *Hesperis matronalis*	Butterflies
Lavatera trimestris	Bees
Poached egg flower *Limnanthes douglasii*	Bees, hoverflies
Honeysuckle *Lonicera periclymenum*	Moths
Honesty *Lunaria annua*	Butterflies
Bergamot *Monarda didyma*	Butterflies, bees
Flowering tobacco *Nicotiana alata*	Moths
Evening primrose *Oenothera biennis*	Butterflies, moths, bees
Marjoram *Origanum majorana*	Butterflies, bees
Alpine poppy *Papaver alpinum*	Hoverflies
Phlox paniculata	Butterflies, moths
Black-eyed Susan *Rudbeckia hirta*	Hoverflies
Sage *Salvia officinalis*	Bees
Iceplant *Sedum spectabile*	Butterflies, bees, hoverflies
Goldenrod *Solidago canadensis*	Bees, hoverflies
African marigold *Tagetes erecta*	Butterflies, bees
French marigold *Tagetes patula*	Butterflies, bees, hoverflies

material to build up a rich, structured, well-aerated soil in the natural way. They don't ruthlessly hack back hedges and shrubs but instead prune and train them in a way that makes best use of their potential. They don't turn to chemicals to exterminate potential pests but instead use cultural methods, mixed planting, encouragement of natural predators, biological control and other management strategies.

The rewards for gardening in as natural a way as possible, with due regard for the normal life processes of plants, are bountiful crops and stunningly attractive ornamentals. The bonus is the pleasure of participating in the interesting lives of the many animals that share our gardens with us. It's absorbing, it enriches the spirit and it feels good.

Preceding page, *frost at Barnsdale. Plants and most animals are dormant in winter and little seems to be happening, although birds and some mammals are active. Come spring, everything will burst into life.*

THE LIVING GARDEN CALENDAR

The following calendar of events taking place in the garden is just
a guide to what is happening and is by no means complete.
As the seasons vary slightly in different years, so does the timing
of flowering, animal breeding and gardening activities.

What's happening in
—January—

Gardening

*Bonfire of accumulated woody, fibrous, thorny and diseased garden rubbish

*Digging cleared flower and vegetable beds

*Harvesting Brussels sprouts and leeks

*Ordering from seed catalogues and planning planting layout

Plants

*Flowers of winter aconites, *Daphne* and Christmas roses appearing

*First snowdrops and early crocuses in flower

*Buds swelling on flowering currants and on *Forsythia*

*Bulbs putting up fat, green spikes

Animals

*Many insects over-wintering as eggs or pupae

*Hedgehogs, bats, amphibians and some adult insects hibernating

*Spiders, centipedes, earthworms, woodlice, etc. slowed down by cold

*Fieldfares and redwings visit to feed on berries

*Well-stocked bird table is especially important

*Squirrels and wood mice are active and conspicuous

*Foxes are courting and mating. High-pitched bark of dog fox can be heard at night.

WHAT'S HAPPENING IN
—FEBRUARY—

Gardening

*Spreading and incorporating compost

*Placing cloches or sheets of plastic to warm soil ready for sowing seeds

Plants

*Crocuses, hardy cyclamen, *Daphne*, *Forsythia*, snowdrops, *Viburnum* and witchhazel in flower

*Myrobalan plum flowers spangle bare twigs

*Fat, red leaf buds of peonies appear

Animals

*Some moth caterpillars feeding, especially angle shades and lesser yellow underwing

*A few moths flying at night

*Holly leaf blotches caused by holly leaf miner become conspicuous

*Greenfinches peck seeds from compost

*Wood pigeons raid budding broccoli

WHAT'S HAPPENING IN
—MARCH—

Gardening

*Dividing herbaceous perennials

*Preparing seed-beds and starting to sow hardy seeds outside, or in greenhouse if you have a slug problem

*Pruning roses

*First lawn cut

*Putting away bird table for summer

Plants

Arabis, Aubrieta, Berberis, flowering currant, daffodils, forget-me-nots, honesty, hyacinths, japonica, magnolia, polyanthus, primroses and scillas in flower

Animals

*Hibernation coming to end

*First butterflies appear

*House sparrows, starlings, blackbirds, thrushes and wrens start nesting

*Fox cubs are born

*Frogs, toads and newts return to ponds

What's happening in
—April—

Gardening

*Getting to grips with weeding whether by hand or hoe

*Sowing more seeds of hardy plants

*Removing old flower-heads from daffodils and other spring bulbs

*Harvesting spring cabbage and first radishes

*Picking first mint

Plants

*Much more greenery in evidence

*Tinge of green starts to show on silver birch, raspberry canes and mock orange

*Ivy-leaved speedwell becomes a troublesome weed

*_Bergenia_, Japanese cherry, grape hyacinths, blue periwinkle, _Phlox drummondii_, rosemary, saxifrage, stocks, tulips and wallflowers in flower

Animals

*First hoverflies

*Honey-bees, bumble-bees and solitary bees are active

*Queen wasps are out of hibernation and searching for nest sites

*Spiders, centipedes, etc. are more active

*Frog and toad spawn appears in ponds

*Blue-tits lay eggs

*Newly-fledged blackbirds and song thrushes appear

*Bullfinches feed on buds on fruit trees

*Tawny owl calls can be heard at night

*Bats and hedgehogs are out of hibernation

WHAT'S HAPPENING IN
—MAY—

Gardening

*Putting up stakes for runner beans and sweet peas

*Planting out greenhouse-grown seedlings of runner beans, sweet peas, etc.

*Sowing seeds of tender plants, such as *Nicotiana*, in greenhouse

*Planting greenhouse tomatoes

*Starting to stake tall herbaceous plants

*Taking softwood cuttings

*Protecting carrots from carrot fly, and cabbages from cabbage root fly

*Hanging codling moth trap in apple tree

*Thinning out pond plants and removing blanketweed

*Harvesting spinach beet

Plants

*Weeds need really keeping under control

*Ferns sprouting tightly-rolled fronds

*Rhubarb and parsley doing well

*Gooseberries begin to develop

*Hops and teazels growing fast

*Broom, columbine, comfrey, crane's-bill, creeping-Jenny, elder, hawthorn, bearded irises, lilac, lilies-of-the-valley, Mexican orange blossom, petunias, rowan and Solomon's seal in flower

Animals

*Nectar-feeding well under way

*More hoverflies appear

*Orange-tip and cabbage white butterflies are active

*Many more moths flying at night, including first hawkmoths

*First workers of bumble-bees and social (yellow) wasps appear

*Solitary bees are conspicuous

*Aphid numbers begin to build up

*More sorts of ladybirds are active

*Cuckoospit appears

*Willow warblers are singing

*Blue-tits are busy collecting food for their nestlings

*Swifts and house martins arrive from Africa

*Hedgehogs courting and mating at night with loud grunting noises

What's happening in
—June—

Gardening

*Starting to plant out tender seedlings, such as African marigolds and courgettes

*Turning over compost heap

*Keeping watch for potential pest problems – hand-picking of caterpillars or rubbing off of aphids helps greatly at this stage

*Making sure your greenhouse is always well-ventilated and plants well-watered

*Regular mowing of grass

*Positioning netting over soft fruit

*Harvesting of strawberries, gooseberries, rhubarb, peas and broad beans

Plants

*First flowers of buddleia and hedge bindweed appear

*Borage, *Convolvulus minor*, *Echium*, elder, *Eschscholtzia*, feverfew, foxgloves, hollyhocks, honeysuckle, lilies, lupins, marigolds, mock orange, peonies, pinks, poppies, sage, thyme-leaved speedwell, sweet peas, valerian, *Weigela* and wisteria in flower

Animals

*Magpie moth caterpillars appear on gooseberry bushes

*Maximum variety of moths seen at night

*First silver-Y moth appears

*Aphid numbers are booming and producing large quantities of honeydew

*Hoverfly larvae are active

*Bumble-bee numbers are at their peak

*Seething clusters of baby garden spiders can be seen

*Bird-song is varied and loud

*House martins are building mud nests beneath house eaves

*Baby bats and hedgehogs are born

*Foxcubs can be spotted out with vixen

WHAT'S HAPPENING IN
—JULY—

Gardening

*Breathing space between the season of sowing and planting and the time of pruning and harvesting

*Dead-heading roses, marigolds, perennial cornflower, buddleia, etc.

Plants

Alstroemeria, clematis, cornflowers, delphiniums, geraniums, *Lavatera*, lavender, yellow loosestrife, mullein, nasturtiums, *Nicotiana*, poached egg flower, *Potentilla fruticosa*, evening primrose, privet, roses and zinnias in flower

Animals

*Large elephant hawk caterpillars with conspicuous eye-markings are to be found on rosebay willowherb and *Fuchsia*

*Solitary wasps peak in numbers and variety

*Winged reproductives of garden black ants swarm from nests

*Birds keep low profile

*Trim *Arabis*, *Aubrieta*, etc.

*First cucumbers and tomatoes ripen in the greenhouse

*Harvesting of raspberries, loganberries and courgettes

*Fledged young birds lurk in vegetation

*Goldfinches eat sage seeds

*Swifts wheel and scream overhead at peak of feeding activity

*Baby frogs move out of pond on to land

*Adult newts shelter beneath vegetation close to pond

*Mole-hills become conspicuous

WHAT'S HAPPENING IN
—AUGUST—

Gardening

*Cutting out old raspberry canes

*Planting out broccoli and wallflower seedlings

*Cutting seed-heads from marguerite daisies

*Summer pruning of trained fruit trees

*Cutting and drying herbs for storage

*Picking runner beans and tomatoes

Plants

*Seeds and 'sharks' teeth' bracts of birch litter paths

*Borage flowers are conspicuous

*Buddleias are in full flower

*Annual asters, *Cosmos*, dahlias, goldenrod, *Helenium*, *Heliopsis*, knapweeds, African and French marigolds, montbretia, *Phlox paniculata*, red-hot pokers, *Rudbeckia*, sweet williams and globe thistles in flower

*Elderberries

Animals

*Butterflies, hoverflies and many other insects peak in numbers

*Immigration of hoverflies to gardens

*Butterflies are to be seen on marjoram flowers

*Green-bottle flies settle on mint flowers

*Crab-spiders appear on flowers

*Wolf spiders are dragging egg sacs

*Orb-webs are conspicuous, especially those of garden spider

*Swifts leave for Africa

*Autumn song of robin can be heard

What's happening in
—September—

Gardening

*Starting to clear fallen leaves

*Lifting, dividing and replanting perennials

Plants

*Herbaceous borders are full of colour

*Chrysanthemums, Michaelmas daisies, ice plant and roses are in flower

*Rose hips are in abundance

*Fennel and lovage seed-heads appear

Animals

*Red admiral, painted lady, peacock and small tortoiseshell butterflies feed at buddleia and ice plant

*Larger hoverflies are conspicuous

*Social (yellow) wasps are abundant, with worker numbers at their peak

*Baby newts leave ponds

*House martins leave for Africa

*Pruning climbing and rambling roses

*Harvesting apples, blackberries and outdoor tomatoes

*Migratory warblers, such as willow warbler, leave the country

*Chiffchaff song can be heard before the birds depart

*Birds begin feeding on fruits and seeds

*Goldfinches feed on teazel seeds

*Greenfinches feed on sunflower seeds

*Bats and hedgehogs are busily feeding up prior to hibernation

What's happening in
—October—

Gardening

*Planting new herbaceous perennials

*Starting taking hardwood cuttings

*Cleaning out greenhouse and removing old tomato and cucumber haulms

*Weeding out *Oxalis* and destroying taproot and bulbils

*Clearing windfall apples on to compost heap

*Harvesting flower seeds for use next year

Plants

*Michaelmas daisies and rest of herbaceous borders start to get raggedy

*Honeysuckle berries appear

*Fungus season begins: toadstools appear on unmown lawns

Animals

*Insect season is nearly over but butterflies, hoverflies and bumble-bees bask in sun on late flowers

*Bumble-bee and wasp nests break up.

Males, workers and old queens die, young queens go into hibernation

*Vast numbers of small, gauzy cobwebs are produced by money spiders

WHAT'S HAPPENING IN
— NOVEMBER —

Gardening

*Planting new trees and shrubs

*Cutting back buddleia and pruning other shrubs

*Pruning bramble

Plants

*Silvery seed-pods of honesty appear

Animals

*Most insects have now started hibernation but there are still a few droneflies (hoverfly) feeding at late flowers

*A few sorts of moths are still flying at night

*Attaching new loganberry stems to fence or support

*Starting to cut down old stalks of perennials

*Sweeping fallen leaves

*Berries of cotoneaster, hawthorn, pyracantha and rowan are conspicuous

*Amphibians go into hibernation

*Starlings probe lawns for leatherjackets, etc.

*Bats and hedgehogs go into hibernation

WHAT'S HAPPENING IN
— DECEMBER —

Gardening

*Protecting delicate plants with cloches or straw

*Mending fences

Plants

*Most plant life is dormant

Animals

*Garden is quiet save for birds, foxes and squirrels

*Winter gnats 'dance' in still afternoon air

*Sharpening lawn-mowers and other tools

*Harvesting Brussels sprouts

*Holly berries are at their best

*Common and black-headed gulls may swoop low over garden

*Well-stocked bird table is important

USEFUL ADDRESSES

English Nature,
Northminster House, Northminster Road,
Peterborough, Cambridgeshire PE1 1UA.
Information on wild flowers, attracting
insects, etc.

Friends of the Earth,
26–28 Underwood Street, London N1 7JQ.
Environmental pressure group.

**Henry Doubleday Research
Association,**
Ryton Gardens, The National Centre for
Organic Gardening, Ryton-on-Dunsmore,
Coventry CV8 3LG.
Information and demonstration gardens on
all aspects of organic gardening. Also
supplies members with most organic
products including seeds, fertilisers and
biological controls.

**National Society of Allotment and
Leisure Gardeners,**
Hunters Road, Corby, Northamptonshire
NN17 1JE
Advice on allotments.

Northern Horticultural Society,
Harlow Carr Botanical Gardens, Crag Lane,
Harrogate, N. Yorkshire HG3 1QB.

Organic Gardening,
PO Box 4, Wiveliscombe, Taunton,
Somerset TA4 2QY.
Monthly journal on organic gardening.

**Royal Caledonian Horticultural
Society,**
3 West Newington Place, Edinburgh EH9
1QT.

Royal Horticultural Society,
Vincent Square, London SW1P 2PE.

Royal Horticultural Society of Ireland,
Thomas Prior House, Merrion Road,
Dublin 4.

Royal Society for Nature Conservation,
The Green, Nettleham, Lincoln LN2 2NR.
Help with native trees and other plants, etc.

Royal Society for the Protection of Birds,
The Lodge, Sandy, Bedfordshire SG19 2DL.
Information and literature on attracting birds, etc.

Soil Association,
86 Colston Street, Bristol BS1 5BB.
Information on organic gardening and farming. The recognised authority on organic standards.

SEEDSMEN

J. W. Boyce,
Bush Pasture, Lower Carter Street, Fordham, Ely, Cambridgeshire CB7 5JU.

John Chambers Wildflower Seeds,
15 Westleigh Road, Barton Seagrave, Kettering, Northamptonshire NN15 5AJ.

Chiltern Seeds,
Bortree Stile, Ulverston, Cumbria LA12 7PB.

Samuel Dobie and Son Ltd,
Broomhill Way, Torquay, Devon TQ2 7QW.

Mr Fothergill's Seeds Ltd,
Gazeley Road, Kentford, Newmarket, Suffolk CB8 7QB.

W. W. Johnson and Son,
London Road, Boston, Lincolnshire PE21 8AD.

S. E. Marshall and Co Ltd,
23/24 Regal Road, Wisbech, Cambridgeshire PE13 2RF.

W. Robinson and Sons,
Sunnybank, Forton, Nr. Preston, Lancashire ER3 0BN.

Suffolk Herbs,
Sawyer Farm, Little Cornard, Sudbury, Suffolk CO10 0NY.

Suttons Seeds Ltd,
Hele Road, Torquay, Devon TQ2 7QJ.

Thompson and Morgan Ltd,
London Road, Ipswich, Suffolk 1P2 0BA

Unwins Seeds Ltd,
Histon, Cambridge CB4 4LE.

GENERAL ORGANIC SUPPLIES

Chase Organic,
Shepperton, Middlesex TW17 8AS.

Cumulus Organics,
Two Mile Lane, Highnam, Gloucestershire GL2 8DW.

Dig and Delve Organics,
Blo Norton, Diss, Norfolk IP22 2BR.

Organic Garden Centre,
Watling Street, Hockliffe, Nr. Leighton Buzzard, Bedfordshire LU7 9NP.

ORGANIC PEST CONTROL

Agralan,
The Old Brickyard, Ashton Keynes, Swindon, Wiltshire SN6 6QR.

Bunting Biological Control Ltd,
The Nurseries, Great Horkesley, Colchester, Essex CO6 4AJ.

English Woodlands Ltd,
Burrow Nursery, Cross in Hand, Heathfield,
E. Sussex TN21 0UG.

Koppert (UK) Ltd,
1 Wadhurst Business Park, Faircrouch
Lane, Wadhurst, E. Sussex TN5 6PT.

Natural Pest Control,
Yapton Road, Barnham, Bognor Regis,
W. Sussex PO22 0BQ.

FRUIT TREES

Deacons Nursery,
Godshill, Isle of Wight PO38 3HW.

Highfield Nurseries,
Whitminster, Gloucestershire GL2 7PL.

SOFT FRUIT

Ken Muir,
Honeypot Farm, Weeley Heath, Clacton-
on-Sea, Essex CO16 9BJ.
Propagator and distributor of certified fruit
stocks. Mail order.

WOODEN GREENHOUSES

Banbury Homes and Gardens,
PO Box 17, Banbury, Oxfordshire OX17
3NS.

S. Wernick & Sons Ltd,
Lindon Road, Brownhills, Walsall,
W. Midlands WS8 7BW

COLD FRAMES

Access Frames,
Crick, Northamptonshire NN6 7BR.

PAVING

ECC Quarries Ltd,
Okus, Swindon, Wiltshire SN1 4JJ

CLAY POTS AND RHUBARB FORCERS

Whichford Potteries,
Whichford, Shipston-on-Stour,
Warwickshire CV36 5PG

FRUIT ARCHES

Agriframes Ltd,
Charlwoods Road, East Grinstead,
W. Sussex RH19 2HG.

PERGOLA KITS

Larch-Lap Ltd,
PO Box 17, Lichfield Street, Stourport-on-
Severn, Worcestershire DY13 9ES.

FURNITURE

Andrew Grace Designs,
51 Bourne Lane, Much Hadham,
Hertfordshire SG10 6ER.

ORNAMENTAL PLANTS

There are, of course, hundreds of nurseries
and garden centres which sell plants. For
particular requirements, we refer you to
The Plant Finder, published by
Headmain Ltd, and the Hardy Plant
Society, Lakeside, Gaines Road,
Whitbourne, Worcestershire WR6 5RD.

INDEX

Page numbers in **italic** *refer to the illustrations and captions*